Collaborative Philanthropies

Collaborative Philanthropies:

What Groups of Foundations Can Do
That Individual Funders Cannot

ELWOOD M. HOPKINS

LEXINGTON BOOKS

Lanham • Boulder • New York • Toronto • Oxford

LEXINGTON BOOKS

Published in the United States of America
by Lexington Books
An imprint of The Rowman & Littlefield Publishing Group, Inc.
4501 Forbes Boulevard, Suite 200, Lanham, Maryland 20706

PO Box 317
Oxford
OX2 9RU, UK

British Library Cataloguing in Publication Information Available

Library of Congress Cataloging-in-Publication Data

Hopkins, Elwood M. (Elwood Morton)
    Collaborative philanthropies : what groups of foundations can do that individual
funders cannot / Elwood M. Hopkins.
        p. cm.
    Includes index.
    ISBN 0-7391-1042-X (cloth : alk. paper) — ISBN 0-7391-1043-8 (pbk. : alk. paper)
    1. Nonprofit organizations—Management. 2. Cooperation. I. Title.
    HD2769.15.H67 2005
    361.7'6—dc22
                                                                        2004025710

Printed in the United States of America

⊖™ The paper used in this publication meets the minimum requirements of
American National Standard for Information Sciences—Permanence of Paper for
Printed Library Materials, ANSI/NISO Z39.48–1992.

This book is dedicated to my parents,
who taught me that both philanthropy
and collaboration begin at home.

CONTENTS

Acknowledgments

Acknowledgments

It can be exhilarating to notice an emerging trend, investigate it through direct interviews and experience, and attempt to describe that trend in writing. For me, this analytical scan of funder collaboratives across the country represented the capturing of just such a trend. And these collaboratives are, in my view, a crucially important trend because they represent models for more effective organized philanthropy, a field that is largely misunderstood and undervalued in modern American society.

When I first began researching funder collaboratives in 1996, it was not as part of a systematic study nor for the preparation of a book. As the newly appointed executive director of Los Angeles Urban Funders (LAUF), I considered it a personal inquiry into other efforts that could help me to do my job better. Along the way, I ventured upon a nationwide group of peers addressing parallel challenges in imaginative ways. I also concluded that funder collaboratives are not just a collection of isolated experiments, but a widespread redefinition of the way grantmaking will be practiced in the twenty-first century.

I am grateful to the many individuals who shared—with rare honesty and humility—their experiences in forming funder collaboratives. Among these, I am particularly indebted to Paul Shoemaker, Kirk Meyer, John Mortimer, Anne Kubisch, Karen Fulbright-Anderson, Cheryl King Fischer, Genie Dixon, Judith K. Chynoweth, Ben Starrett, Alison De Lucca, Maximo Cuellar, Lynn Lohr, Elizabeth Bremner, Barbara Poppe, Catherine Porter, Robert Sherman, Tracey Rutnik, Alice Eason Jenkins, Jamaica Maxwell, Jonathan Spack, Maria Rogers Pascual, Jennifer Vannica, Cheryl Hayes, Valerie Wright, Julie Meenan, Walt Florie, John Williams, David La Piana, Diana Campoamor, Barbara Gebhard, Beverly Coleman, and Kim Burnett.

The members of Los Angeles Urban Funders (LAUF), the collaborative I have staffed for more than eight years, have been my closest learning companions. My experiences with these individuals, more than any others, were formative in my views on funder collaboratives, and this book draws upon my work with them more heavily than with any other collaborative. Lon Burns, the president of the Southern California Grantmakers at LAUF's inception—and in a real sense, a father to LAUF—was my earliest guide, and he created a learning-based environment in which my work could grow.

Among LAUF members, I am particularly grateful to Caroline Boitano, Carolyn Brooks, Jan Bryant, Dannielle Campos, James Canales, Dennis Collins, Pat Christopher, Vera De Vera, Leslie Dorman, Patrick Escobar, Shirley Fredricks, Sukey Garcetti, Craig Howard, Ken Gregorio, Maritza Guzman, Chet Hewitt, Bonnie Guiton-Hill, Beverly Hoskinson, Chi Hughes, Fran Jemmott, Eric Johnson, Stewart Kwoh, Deborah Lewis, Julia Lopez, Cassandra Malry, Antonio Manning, Jan McCoy Miller, Craig McGarvey, Michele Myszka, Torie Osborn, Miyoko Oshima, Claire Peeps, Janice Pober, Michele Prichard, Dr. Robert Ross, Russell Sakaguchi, Jack Shakely, Judy Spiegel, Wendy Wachtell, Jonathan Weedman, Dr. DarEll Weist, Dr. Ralph Williams, Amelia Xann, Gary Yates, and Teri Yeager.

Jan McElwee, the lead consultant to LAUF since its inception, has been a close colleague, sage advisor, constructive critic, and big sister to me throughout my tenure at LAUF. She, along with the other LAUF consultants, Dr. Julia Solis, Dr. Morgan Lyons, Dr. Susan Philliber, Dr. Cheryl Grills, Dr. Denise Fairchild, Cecilia Sandoval, Mary Lee, Lisa Nichols, Rudeen Monte, and Rigo Orozco, were extraordinary classmates in this educational process. Sylvia Castillo, who spent a yearlong fellowship working side by side with me in 1999, generously shared her fresh and forthright perspectives on philanthropy.

The ideas in this book have been shaped in the context of several extended dialogues, especially the Harvard Executive Session on the Future of Philanthropy, which met twice yearly from 1999 to 2002, and the Marco Polo discussion series convened by Marcia Sharp from 2000 to 2002, as well as ongoing dialogues of the Aspen Institute Roundtable on Comprehensive Community Initiatives. Moreover, my conclusions were shaped at more than two dozen conferences hosted by regional associations, affinity groups, and local foundations nationwide. Among my principal mentors, teachers, and colleagues in these sessions have been Christine Letts, Joel Fleishman, Ed Skloot, Paul Brest, Ralph Smith, Ralph Hamilton, Miriam Shark, Marcia Sharp, Peggy Dulany, Peter Frumkin, Lucy Bernholz, Michael Shuman, Jim Ferris, and, above all, Shirley Fredricks and Dennis Collins, whom I credit with introducing me to philanthropy in the first place.

It was Gabriel Kasper and his associates at the Packard Foundation who originally saw the potential for this book, funded the preparation of the manuscript, and financed its publication. I am truly indebted to them. Equally important, Gabriel was the critical and supportive friend that every author needs when embarking on the writing of a book. Mark Sedway at the Williams Group was an expert adviser in helping to ensure the book's relevance to specific audiences. And it was John

Hurliman who assisted me every day for two years in sorting, organizing, and typing my handwritten notes; coordinating my interviews; and overseeing the finalization of the text. He has been an outstanding partner in this endeavor.

R. Christine Hershey, the president of Hershey Associates/Cause Communications, along with her creative team members Kristin Allen, Andrew Posey, and Linda Apeles, provided invaluable guidance and vision in conceptualizing the book, designing its final product, and overseeing a masterful marketing and dissemination strategy.

Finally, on a personal note, I would like to thank Craig Zadan, for his support and inspiration in all areas of my life, and my friends Michael Green and Daniel Tellalian, who backed me up as only good friends can do.

Elwood M. Hopkins
Los Angeles, California
February 2004

CHAPTER 1

Funder Collaboratives in Context: Philanthropy as a Professional Field

Philanthropy stands at a defining moment. It is poised to either evolve to its next stage as a professional field, or not.

Every professional field shares certain characteristics. These typically include a sense of purpose and a set of specific roles to perform in society; common standards and practices; mechanisms for training, educating, and cultivating leaders; an infrastructure of institutions and peer networks; codes of professional behavior and conduct; and a fundamental capacity for different organizations to work together in setting agendas and achieving objectives.

The latter characteristic is particularly relevant to this book.[1] A professional field cannot exist without collaborative or cooperative arrangements among institutions that exploit interdependencies and combine resources for the purpose of enhancing their accomplishments. Moreover, a field needs to be able to centralize and pool financial resources if it is to mount large-scale strategies and initiatives. Collaboratives, broadly defined, are an indication of a mature professional field.

In business, corporations come together in conglomerates or mergers, combining and recombining in order to yield higher profits or gain competitive advantage. Trade associations, merchant groups, and business improvement districts are smaller-scale examples of businesses coming together to pool resources and take collective action. Similarly, in government, public agencies establish systems for interdepartmental coordination and chains of command among federal, state, and local authorities. At a grassroots level, political constituency groups form and re-form alliances in order to achieve public policy objectives.

In the independent sector, however, talk of collaboration seems quaint by comparison. There has been a growing body of research and practice related to strategic restructuring among nonprofit organizations. But discussion of funder collaboration is a new phenomenon, tentative at best. And in truth, we cannot expect nonprofits to firmly embrace collaboration until the funders of their work embrace it. Because philanthropy lacks these arrangements, it has held back the effectiveness of the entire sector.

Many have argued that philanthropy can never constitute a professional field in the sense that medicine, education, journalism, or law does. They point out that individual funders have nothing in common other than tax codes—and perhaps a vague sense of "giving back" to society. Each foundation has its own style, interest areas, governance mechanisms, and ways of operating. And most importantly, funders do not generally understand themselves as part of a system. In a way, philanthropy can be considered a "pre-system," since foundations have not as yet demonstrated evolutionary behaviors that benefit the whole field.

This is not to say that there is no extensive inherited infrastructure upon which a professional field can be built. There is the national Council on Foundations and its subsidiary affinity groups, the regional associations and their national forum, and the foundation libraries and their national network. There are a handful of research institutes dedicated partially or fully to the study of philanthropic trends and practices; and there are national periodicals like *Foundation News and Commentary* or *The Chronicle on Philanthropy*. Furthermore, the Council on Foundations, the Philanthropic Initiative, and a number of research institutes and resource centers are raising explicit questions about the need for professional standards for the field.

But philanthropy's institutions rarely transcend open-ended networking or academic exchanges of information. They stop short of exercising any proactive leadership. As a result, they have little success in helping funders to embrace notions of "teaming" or working together on shared agendas. Within current systems of regional associations and affinity groups, some ideas do surface and predominate; but were there proper organizational structures and ongoing dialogues in place, these ideas could serve as a basis for concerted action. In short, if philanthropy is to become more effective as a field, it will need to develop an infrastructure that will catalyze collaboration. It will need to be able to intentionally create change within itself.

The good news is that fields can, and do, change over time. Jacques Barzun has deduced that professions are dynamic, vulnerable, and inherently unstable. He explains this changing character by distinguishing between a profession and a function. "The function may well be eternal, such as the act of giving. But the profession, which is the cluster of practices and relationships arising from the function at a given time or place, can be destroyed—or even destroy itself—very rapidly."[2] If philanthropic leaders remain focused on their function in society, then inefficient practices and relationships will fall away of their own accord, to be replaced by new, more adaptive ones.

In this spirit, it is worth unbundling the internal barriers that prevent philanthropy from fulfilling its potential as a field. Three of the most important barriers include extreme diversity, lack of accountability, and the absence of meaningful professional standards. Each of these can be examined in turn.

Diversity

A primary obstacle to philanthropy's ability to function as a field is also one of its celebrated strengths: the sheer diversity of its members. Philanthropy has grown enormously in recent years and with that growth has come a stunning diversification of philanthropic structures and funding mechanisms. Today, there are a multitude of financial structures through which money is removed from the economic markets of labor and consumerism, or the ongoing cycle of taxation and public expenditure, in order to be set aside for the public good. The particular organizational forms and financial instruments have become more diverse over time. Correspondingly, the process of deciding how money is spent and who is involved in decision making varies enormously.

In addition to large, private foundations and corporate contributions departments, there are employee funds; high school foundations and scholarship funds; community bank trusts; funds managed by investment companies or brokerage houses; funds under the direction of churches, synagogues, fraternities, sororities, and social clubs; family foundations; donor-advised funds (typically managed in the aggregate at community foundations); federated funds that collect resources and redistribute them to others; civic groups like the Junior League or Rotary; and trade associations that organize grantmaking programs. There are ethnic funds, legal compensation and reparation funds, lending circles, land trusts, and operating foundations.

Some argue that promoting diversity is in itself the purpose of the field. They argue, not incorrectly, that foundations cultivate plurality, expressiveness, and innovation without which there can be no true open society. Funders, they submit, must seek those strategies that will ensure ongoing creativity in addressing problems and seeking participation. If donors lack substantive or stylistic commonalities, it is because they have appropriately placed value on individual expression and the promotion of dispersed power centers, or polyarchies. Far from being a problem to be solved, it is a force for reinventing democracy.

But while our differences can be a great strength, they inevitably complicate our collective thought process. Funders work in a range of situations and institutions of different sizes, missions, and operating styles, which means they have to work hard to find the crosscutting issues and points of collaboration. Moreover, foundation leaders sometimes prize idiosyncrasies and individuality at the expense of basic group norms. In this field, we can witness a clash of egos whenever someone attempts to exert leadership. At its worst, it is a "Wild West world" in which there are few legitimized leadership ladders and in which competitive energies are frequently unchanneled.

Accountability

In addition to the challenges of diversity, there is an utter lack of accountability that might otherwise drive funders to congregate in achieving outcomes and establish standards and practices that would enhance their effectiveness. Private foundations are insulated from taxpayer and interest group pressures. Unfettered by consumer market demands, shareholder interests, or the imperatives of cost savings and profit making, they are subject to none of the external forces that necessitate self-organization in other sectors. Philanthropy, for better and for worse, is basically accountable to no one.

Philanthropy's independence should be protected and preserved because it is a unique attribute relative to business or government. Private grantmakers, relative to their counterparts in other fields, can take more risks and be more situational, strategic, and nimble in their investments. They also possess the perpetuity that allows them to stay with long-term agendas that surpass quarterly earnings reports, short-term product life cycles, or terms of political office. As funders of many different efforts, foundations can use their panoramic vantage point to support the overall nonprofit infrastructure and its crosscutting needs. And they can generate heterogeneity in solutions to societal problems.

But maximizing these collective advantages, relative to other sectors such as business and government, requires a level of cohesion. Only an organized philanthropic field can possibly hope to interact in a significant way with the organized fields of business and government. Philanthropy will never realize its full potential unless it utilizes these unique traits and freedoms, and mobilizes and aggregates its resources to do so. And that will involve developing a collective sense of accountability, or at least a workable mechanism for external feedback.

If philanthropy is not to be assessed from without, then it at least needs information that can be used to determine its own success or failure and also to improve performance. Ideally, these systems would be shared, whenever possible, in such a way that new standards of practice would arise along with productive peer pressure and group norms.

Professional Standards

One of the basic building blocks of any professional field is a set of commonly accepted standards that can help in evaluating performance and defining excellence. Standards do not need to be viewed as dogmatic—in fact, quite the opposite: they function as a framework for continuous evaluation and improvement.

Though it may sound innocuous, the creation of professional standards is a highly political and usually contentious process. Asserting one standard usually involves displacing another. The adoption of Western medical standards, for example, has suppressed Eastern and holistic medical practices. In the United States, educational standards prioritize reading, writing, mathematics, and science over the arts and humanities.

How did other fields develop standards and practices? Many were driven to do so by an awareness of the harms they might face were they *not* to do so. Medicine, for example, can cause injury or death to someone if administered improperly. It was a worrisome drop-off in skills within the U.S. labor pool that triggered the "back-to-basics" movement in American school standards. But in philanthropy, most people are sanguine. Funders silently assure themselves, "We're giving away money. How can we do harm?"

Recently, the Council on Foundations began working on a set of professional standards that would be widely accepted by grantmakers. Appropriately, these standards focus less on substantive content than on basic tools and mechanics such as appropriate salary ranges for foundation personnel, prototype formats for proposals, site-visit etiquette, and protocols for due diligence. The Independent Sector recently began promoting a "Model Code of Ethics" for nonprofits and foundations. But even with a set of standards in hand, enforcement is problematic. It is hard to imagine peer review panels of funders traveling around the country to assess a particular foundation's adherence to standards, as we see in school or hospital accreditation.

And it would be difficult to imagine how grantees would learn about these standards or how they would respond were the standards not met. As it is, grantees learn about philanthropic practices in an ad lib fashion, based on accumulated experience with multiple funders. Through trial and error, they learn about what constitutes a legitimate grantee or due diligence. But efficient donor-grantee relations call for some basic standards and expectations, and collaborative action among funders requires some shared acceptances about what constitutes good practice.

Field Building for Philanthropy

Finding points of commonality amid diversity, constructing shared accountabilities, and agreeing on professional standards are all steps along the path to the growth of a professional field. But philanthropy is by no means destined to head in this direction.

It is true that private foundations, including Packard, Hewlett, Irvine, Ford, Rockefeller, Surdna, Kellogg, and Kauffman, have been addressing these challenges through grantmaking initiatives aimed at strengthening the linkages between community foundations and their partners, expanding the services of regional associations, and underwriting foundation conferences or research projects. But they continually face a pernicious counterargument: that funders should not "self-deal" by investing in any strategy to improve the philanthropic field.

More specifically, funder collaboratives come under fire. The transactional costs of setting up and staffing collaboratives are sometimes viewed as yet another bureaucratic apparatus and a waste of resources that could otherwise flow directly to nonprofits and the clients they serve. As experiments, funder collaboratives will certainly fail from time to time, but to not invest in their development will most certainly hold philanthropy back. In fact, this fear of investing in the philanthropic field threatens to become the most significant barrier to the effectiveness of foundations everywhere.

If philanthropy is to become more effective as a field in producing social returns, its members will need to come together more often in groupings, collaboratives, or camps that consolidate their efforts toward common outcomes where appropriate. If we accept that philanthropy is a pre-system that is moving toward becoming some sort of professional field, collaborative dialogue will be the only way to sift through differences and similarities and to identify the points where foundations can be unified by some basic principles and practices.

Collaboration will also be the only way to truly harvest the benefits of those areas where foundations are truly different from one another. It will serve as a platform for diverse expressions of generosity, humanity, and progress. Collaboratives and networks of diverse funders can serve as vehicles for helping foundations to define specializations in relation to one another based on relative strengths. For such collaboratives, the challenge is about managing member differences and discovering productive new synergies that will unleash the full potential of philanthropy as a source of change in modern society.

Fortunately, as chapter 2 will illustrate, there is ample reason for optimism.

Notes

1. The ideas in this chapter took shape during the Harvard Executive Session on the Future of Philanthropy, a three-year extended conversation among foundation executives convened by the Hauser Center at Harvard's Kennedy School of Government.
2. Barzun, Jacques. "The Professions under Siege: Private Practice versus Public Need." *Harper's Magazine* 257 (October 1978): 61-67.

CHAPTER 2

A Tentative Trend:
Illustrative Examples of Funder Collaboratives

While foundations have historically demonstrated little inclination to collaborate, there are now quite a few collaboratives to look at and talk about. As this chapter will illustrate, funder collaboration—though still the exception—is happening with enough frequency to be called a trend. Funder collaboratives, despite all odds, are growing in number, size, and sophistication.[1]

These collaboratives are more than just isolated enterprises. They are increasingly networked with one another, and there has been a reasonably good transfer of knowledge from one collaborative experiment to the next. Newer funder collaboratives have tended to start where the first ones left off, by conferring with the funders of the earlier effort. In California, for instance, the Los Angeles Urban Funders (LAUF) built itself on the experience of a failed funder collaborative, the East Bay Funders (EBF), drawing important lessons that enabled LAUF to enjoy a longer, more fruitful life than its predecessor. The honest and unedited sharing of EBF's experiences with LAUF was an unusual and pivotal ingredient to LAUF's eventual successes. The LAUF, in turn, has passed its learnings on to newer collaboratives in San Diego and Long Beach.

Collaboration can mean many things, of course, and these efforts can vary enormously. Too often, while a group of multiple foundations may be referred to as a collaborative, it can rarely be considered truly consortial. But a growing number of foundations are willing to compromise their autonomy in true partnership with other foundations. According to participants, their purpose is not only to prevent duplication, but to share financial risks and concentrate a wider range of staff expertise and time on complex problems. Collaboration also promises more political muscle, which may be necessary to secure political support for a given initiative or to attract public sector co-funding. Finally, collaboration diversifies funding streams, making the initiative more sustainable.

As Lucy Bernholz explains, "Foundations are both independent and interdependent institutions. They are still products of individuals, families, or corporations that wish to stand recognized for their unique contributions. They still manage their portfolios separately, hire individual staffs, perform their own (often repetitive and redundant) due diligence on grants, and publish their own reports on the impact of their grants. Yet they increasingly operate within loose associations, the growing density of like organizations has not been lost on them, and there is frequent talk of networks of funders and partnerships with grantees."[2]

What follows are brief synopses of over forty funder collaboratives from across the country:

- **The Social Venture Partners** (SVP) is a funder pool that seeks to develop individual philanthropy and volunteerism to achieve positive social change in the Puget Sound Region, with a focus on children and youth (in or out of school) and the environment. Individual "investors" contribute a minimum of $5,500 annually for at least two years. These investors may then collaborate with each other through structured volunteer teams to directly assist SVP investors. The collaborative structure allows for a level of staffing and institutional support that no one donor could afford on his own.

- **The Boston Schoolyard Initiative**: In 1994, the Boston GreenSpace Alliance and the Urban Land Use Task Force approached the city of Boston to initiate a dialogue about the poor condition of Boston's public schoolyards and the possibility of public/private cooperation to revitalize these neglected spaces. The mayor convened a broad-based Schoolyard Task Force to devise a process that would fund projects and help hasten their completion. The Boston Schoolyard Initiative was formally launched in 1995. The city of Boston has committed $2 million a year to fund improvements to school grounds. The Boston Department of Neighborhood Development provides project management and oversees the services of contracted landscape architects. The Boston Schoolyard Funders Collaborative and other private sector partners have contributed over $3 million to the initiative. Private dollars have funded capital improvements as well as grants for community organizing, professional development for educators, and maintenance/sustainability awards to Schoolyard Groups.

- **AIDS Partnership California** is a project of Northern California Grantmakers, with nine foundations pooling funding for HIV prevention, capacity building, public policy, and care and treatment efforts. Formed in 1988 as the AIDS Task Force, it was a response to the escalating HIV epidemic in the San Francisco Bay Area, expanding statewide in 2000. The partnership has awarded over $9 million since its inception. Examples of current grantmaking include building the capacity of nonprofit organizations to provide

AIDS prevention and care services, strengthening public policy efforts at the state level, and demonstrating effective HIV prevention interventions for people of color with HIV. The Partnership's Advisory Committee includes representatives from foundations, the University of California, and the California State Office of AIDS.

- **The Aspen Institute Roundtable on Community Change** was established in 1992 to keep track of the then-emerging field of comprehensive community initiatives and related innovations in inner-city revitalization. Formerly known as the Aspen Institute Roundtable on Comprehensive Community Initiatives, the Roundtable captures and distills lessons about community change efforts and the policies and practices that affect them. A consortium of private foundations provides support for the Roundtable's work. Its funding partners have at times included two federal agencies, and its members include foundation officers, public officials, community-based leaders, and other experts in the field.

- **The San Diego Neighborhood Funders** is a collaborative that has pooled funds at the United Way of San Diego in order to support large-scale community development in the Market Creek section of San Diego. The collaborative has administered a range of funding strategies, including minigrants and facilitated planning efforts. A primary purpose is to create a community of funders that possess an in-depth familiarity with this neighborhood, and so there is an emphasis on events and activities that bring funders together with neighborhood residents and leaders.

- **The Summer Fund Donor Collaborative** was started in 1971 to address the critical need for summer programs for low-income urban youth from Boston, Cambridge, Chelsea, and Somerville. Close to fifty foundations and corporations participate in the Collaborative. In 2003, a total of seventy organizations served 14,800 youth with $1.4 million in operational and programmatic support raised through the Summer Fund. The strength of the Summer Fund lies in its capacity to be both a collaboration of donors and a collaborative of nonprofits. Both groups working together meet one common goal: to provide high-quality, affordable extracurricular programs to urban youth during the summer months. The Summer Fund has several special initiatives to support summer camps.

- **The West Palm Beach Neighborhood Funders Collaborative** is housed at the United Way of Dade County, Florida. This collaborative of fifteen public and private funders pools its resources in support of neighborhood development efforts in three low-income Everglades communities. The Collaborative received startup assistance from the John D. and Catherine T. MacArthur Foundation, and then, with deliberation, assembled funders representing diverse areas of expertise required to address the complex problems of the communities.

- **The New England Grassroots Environment Fund** (NEGEF) was started by four foundations in response to calls from the regional environmental community. The Fund's purpose is to empower local residents, groups, and others to become activists and vocal citizens engaged in environmental stewardship. Nearly half of their grants go to ad hoc groups without 501(c)3 status, and two-thirds of all grantees have no staff. Most groups are either all-volunteer led or have only part-time staff positions. Twenty-three local and regional foundations participated in the collaborative in 2003. The NEGEF is governed by a board and grantmaking committee of activists and funding partners. Most of the grantees cannot be funded by the foundations individually because they fall outside the definitions of formal nonprofits.

- **The Minnesota Futures Fund** was established in 1995 in response to federal budget cuts and devolution on local nonprofit organizations. Its goal was to enable nonprofits to provide effective services in the context of major policy changes. The Fund leveraged three statewide membership organizations—the Minnesota Council on Foundations, the Minnesota Council of Nonprofits, and the Minnesota Council of Churches—as well as thirty-nine grantmakers and the state of Minnesota, to create a $2 million pooled fund. This fund provided an opportunity for the nonprofits to take time away from business as usual to assess the impact of devolution welfare reform and potential budget cuts on their organizations and those they serve. Many nonprofits revised their mission statements and restructured their working relations with other organizations. Some redesigned their fundraising plans, increased their resources through improved use of volunteers, or developed new sources of revenue. Few of the foundations could have released funds for such open-ended purposes.

- **The Foundation Consortium for California's Children and Youth** is an alliance of seventeen corporate, private, community, and family foundations that share a common vision for California's children, families, and communities. They are a nonpartisan resource, bringing philanthropy together with community, schools, and government to improve public policy and practice. The Foundation Consortium influences policy development and implementation at the state, county, and community levels. They do this so that California's children can be safe, healthy, and learning each day. Many of the individual funders are prohibited from carrying out advocacy activities on their own, but are able to do it collaboratively through the intermediary of the Consortium. Styled as a behind-the-scenes player, it is oriented toward improving state policies and systems in California and making the community-based approach the standard for all systems serving children and their families.

- **The Funders' Network for Smart Growth and Livable Communities** serves as an active resource and focal point for foundations, nonprofit organizations, and other partners working to solve the environmental, social, and economic problems created by suburban sprawl and urban disinvestment. The Funders' Network informs and networks funders, shares effective strategies and tools, builds the capacity of key constituencies to promote smart growth and livable communities, and raises awareness about the interdisciplinary nature of these issues and the need for sustained engagement by a diverse coalition of funders. Like the Foundation Consortium, the Funders' Network serves a critical function by positioning its members to help shape policy agendas they could not take on alone.

- **The Los Angeles Immigrant Funders Collaborative** was established in 2000 by a group of local and regional funders to increase philanthropic response to needs of immigrants and refugees in Los Angeles County. Nearly $1.2 million in grants have been made over the past three years to immigrant-based or immigrant-serving organizations that are working in areas such as healthcare, education, civic participation, and economic development. The aim of the Collaborative is to engage both funders that have historically supported immigrant needs and funders that do grantmaking in areas such as health, children and youth, and community development but whose grants to date have not reflected a targeted inclusion of immigrant needs. Recognizing the vital role that immigrant-based organizations play and the enormous contributions they make to their communities, the Collaborative seeks to strengthen the capacity and build the long-term viability of immigrant-based organizations. The Collaborative focuses on small, emerging organizations.

- **Living Cities (formerly the National Community Development Initiative)** is a national nonprofit partnership that provides financial support to nonprofit community development corporations (CDCs) with the goal of revitalizing cities and improving the lives of people in distressed urban neighborhoods. Living Cities's membership is made up of major national foundations, financial institutions, and federal agencies, with these organizations providing their time and resources to invest collaboratively in twenty-three cities around the country. Members of the board of directors include foundation presidents, senior corporate leadership, and senior federal officials. From its inception, Living Cities has invested through two primary intermediaries, the Local Initiatives Support Corporation (LISC) and the Enterprise Foundation.

- **The Consultative Group on Biological Diversity (CGBD)** is a grantmakers' forum that seeks to focus attention on issues and program opportunities related to the conservation and restoration of biological resources. Established in 1987, the CGBD is now comprised of fifty foundations and the U.S. Agency for International Development. The CGBD is funded by program grants from its members and is supported by both full-time and part-time staff. The secretariat serves as a resource and catalyst—providing information, generating ideas, and connecting foundations that share common grantmaking agendas. The CGBD is organized into working groups, and subgroups, to target attention on selected topics and to explore the process of strategic, collaborative grantmaking. Current working groups include forest conservation, conservation of marine biodiversity, biodiversity and environmental health, and climate and energy.

- **The Community Shelter Board (CSB)** was established in 1986 in response to the growing problem of homelessness in Columbus, Ohio. CSB initially focused on a streamlined funding process and general long-term system planning for the homeless services field. While hands-on involvement from philanthropic and government funders was essential during this visioning and planning phase, The CSB now operates as an independent nonprofit organization that coordinates most of the private and public funding for homelessness in the county. Trustees serving on the CSB are appointed by funders, but these trustees are neither foundation staff nor representatives of homeless service agencies. Local funders include the Columbus Foundation, the Leo Yassenoff Foundation, and the city of Columbus. Service providers apply directly to CSB for funds, rather than to the original funding sources, and the CSB board votes on allocation decisions.

- **The Global Catalyst Foundation** was established as an outgrowth of an investment company. A portion of returns from one of the investment funds was directed into the Foundation. Staff of the Foundation typically brief the company's multitude of investors on the programs being funded, and these investors often co-fund these programs. At one point, the Foundation issued an RFP and received sixty proposals, which staff narrowed down to twenty. Foundation staff only had sufficient resources for ten, so they invited a group of individual investors to act as a funding board and to decide which ten programs would be funded. This group of donors decided that all twenty programs should be funded, so one of them wrote a personal check to finance the remaining ten programs. The significance of this approach to governance is that the Foundation board delegates its decision making to a group of other donors. By enlisting a group of investors in the Foundation decision making, this process engaged them on behalf of their own grantmaking and created alignment between the various funding streams.

- **The Funders Forum on Antibiotic Resistance** is an informal strategic alignment of funders working in partnership with a coalition of nonprofit organizations. These funders first came together within the Health and Environmental Funders Network with the goal of reducing or eliminating the use of antibiotics in agriculture. Led by the Joyce Foundation, the Funders Forum gave a group of grantees a sum of money and suggested that they explore ways of working together. The grantees self-organized and presented their collective strategy back to the Joyce Foundation. Joyce, in turn, invited a group of other funders to form the Funders Forum, a group that now supports the national nongovernmental organizations in a working partnership on antibiotic resistance issues.

- **The Funders' Collaborative on Youth Organizing** was established to create a funding stream that would support youth-organizing activities as well as a wide range of advocacy and pressure campaigns around issues that may not usually fit squarely within categorical funding guidelines, such as public safety, educational reform, juvenile justice, the environment, and welfare reform. All participating funders believe that youth organizing is a critical area for increased funding because it helps focus youth action and attention on important systemic social problems while at the same time building important skills for participation in our democracy. And by participating in youth organizing, foundations begin to understand the impacts they have on individual youth development, organizational change, and concrete policy reforms that are the central goals of these efforts. The Collaborative also helps foundations learn how these largely nontraditional organizations do, in fact, fit in with established foundation guidelines and programs.

- **The National Rural Funders Collaborative** (NRFC) was founded to address the paucity of philanthropic resources that flow in rural communities and to create funding streams that would support collaborative efforts among nonprofits in rural geographies—and then network these collaborative initiatives in order to promote learning among them. The NRFC is also committed to attracting other funding to these initiatives by declaring them "opportunities to watch." Some of the initiatives that have been developed with support of the NRFC include providing new sources of capital for promoting sustainable agriculture and forestry, new financial products for low-income residents of rural areas, cooperative models for rural economic development, and new small-scale local philanthropies in Appalachia, Georgia, Mississippi, Minnesota, Montana, Louisiana, and numerous Native American reservations.

- **The Health Funders Partnership of Orange County** was formed as a way for nine local funders to leverage their resources by launching systemic initiatives around major health issues that none could address alone. As its initial endeavor, the Partnership launched a $2.4 million Diabetes Initiative with two goals: to put in place processes for small and mid-size funders to work together to address locally identified health priorities, and to demonstrate some replicable models for bringing together a comprehensive array of health interventions to address a chronic health problem.

- **The Neighborhood 2000 Fund** is a pooled fund committed to growing the capacity of small neighborhood-based organizations, most of which have housing as one of their core issues. With thirty-one member foundations, the collaborative is a mix of local and national funders, about half of which are corporate. Each member has one vote, regardless of the amount of his contribution. The New York Community Trust serves as the fiscal agent for the pool, as a donor-advised fund. Group decision making happens through a subcommittee structure that feeds into the larger collaborative.

- **The Commonweal Marin County Funder Consortium on Antibiotics** was formed after the Joyce Foundation funded a group of nonprofits to self-organize and carry out a large-scale collaborative initiative. Once this initiative was framed and underway, a funder collaborative was organized for the purpose of assembling the diverse array of funding streams required to underwrite the initiative that the nonprofits had designed. Interestingly, the funder collaborative had set aside a small sum of money in case they did not like what the nonprofits devised, but they haven't needed it.

- **The Baltimore Neighborhood Collaborative** (BNC), established in 1995, is a way for local foundations and corporate giving programs to take a more coordinated approach to building stronger communities in Baltimore and the region. BNC members believe that they can increase their impact as individual grantmakers and attract new funders to community development through mutual learning, collective action, and joint grantmaking. To date, BNC has awarded over $2 million to support the capacity of twelve organizations engaged in comprehensive community development, neighborhood planning, and community organizing work encompassing fifty Baltimore neighborhoods. BNC also hosts and sponsors community forums to encourage diverse groups to share information and coordinate activity related to community development.

- **The Southern Funders Collaborative** is an alliance between three philanthropic entities: the Fund for Southern Communities, which raises funds from foundations and individuals and regrants them to support grassroots organizing and social change in North Carolina, South Carolina, and Georgia; the Appalachian Community Fund, which provides grants to groups promoting progressive change in Central Appalachia (East Tennessee, Eastern Kentucky,

Southwest Virginia, and West Virginia); and the Southern Partners Fund, a public foundation created by grantee partners of the Bert and Mary Meyer Foundation. Seeded by the Ford Foundation, these three funders have pooled resources to provide capacity-building grants and technical assistance to nonprofits in a dozen states across the South.

- **The Funders for Sustainable Food Systems** (FSFS) is a California-based group of public and private grantmakers whose mission is to promote sustainable food systems in California that protect the environment, human health, and the welfare of animals. The group's vision embraces all parts of an economically viable food sector and calls for just conditions and fair compensation for farmers, fishers, and workers. FSFS also aims to provide all people with locally produced, affordable, and healthy food. The funders see this as a way to contribute to the vitality of rural and urban communities and the links between them. FSFS has a vision of California as the leader and model state developing sustainable food systems. It works toward this vision by raising funder awareness about the critical need for, and the multiple problem areas addressed by, sustainable food systems. To FSFS, areas such as public health, environmental degradation, labor rights, marine ecosystems, animal welfare, and food security are innately linked to the way food is grown, distributed, and consumed in California. FSFS convenes grantmakers from various sectors as a forum to work together and identify opportunities for systemic solutions.

- **The Roots of Change Fund** (ROC Fund) is a nine-member funder collaborative that emerged and separated from FSFS in 2003 and is now a project of the Trust for Conservation Innovation. It aims to accelerate the transition to sustainable food systems by increasing the human and financial resources devoted to this issue, strengthen this emerging field, and support work toward system change. The goal of the ROC Fund is to transform California food systems by making high-leverage grants. The ROC Fund is advised by the Roots of Change Council, an advisory board of food and agriculture experts representing multiple sectors of the food system. To date, they have funded the AG Innovations Network to carry out food system priorities in two California counties: Ecotrust, to prepare a blueprint for a sustainable food system in California, and the Natural Resources Defense Council, to bring together policy makers and community leaders to begin framing new statewide policies.

- **The New Haven Capacity Building Funders Collaborative** is a special initiative of Third Sector New England. It was established to provide a range of technical assistance, capacity building, and training activities to nonprofits in the Greater New Haven area. These include a research resource group, a leadership institute, organizational development assessments, peer learning opportunities, core funding, and venture capital. This project is expected to have an impact not only on the effectiveness and power of individual nonprofits, but on the effectiveness and power of the whole system of nonprofits in this region.

- **Local Initiative Funding Partners** (LIFP) is a partnership program between the Robert Wood Johnson Foundation and local foundations that aggregates funding for innovative, community-based health initiatives serving vulnerable populations. The process is initiated when a local funder or group of funders proposes a funding partnership with the Robert Wood Johnson Foundation around a specific project that is consistent with the Foundation's guidelines and priorities. Applications are filed by the local collaborative and are then subject to a competitive review process at the Foundation. LIFP provides grants of up to $500,000 for each selected project, which must be matched dollar for dollar by local community foundations, family foundations, or corporate grantmakers. The total award is paid out over a three-year or four-year period.

- **The Racial Justice Collaborative** is a group of funders committed to addressing racial discrimination with strategies that go beyond strictly legal solutions. The Collaborative was created in response to the Rockefeller Foundation's report, *Louder Than Words: Lawyers, Communities, and the Struggle for Justice,* which revealed the persistence of structural racism despite the advances of the civil rights movement. The Collaborative is made up of three funding initiatives: a national grantmaking fund; state and regional grantmaking funds; and a documentation and learning initiative. The Collaborative promotes innovative solutions that bring legal resources and perspectives to grassroots groups working in areas as diverse as education, healthcare access, housing, and employment.

- **The Los Angeles Urban Funders** (LAUF) is a collaborative that was formed after the 1992 civil unrest in Los Angeles. This consortium of thirty foundations pooled funds at the Southern California Grantmakers and has met monthly to allocate these funds to three low-income geographic areas. These pooled funds can be used flexibly to underwrite all of the facilitation, networking, training, leadership development, and management assistance required to set up a comprehensive initiative in each community. Each foundation then funds participating agencies individually through their categorical guidelines.

- **The Long Beach Funders** is a funder collaborative comprised of six foundations that existed in Long Beach, California, from 1996 to 2003. Made up of executives and senior program officers from both small local foundations and larger institutions, the group collectively designed, funded, and monitored a local workforce initiative called "908LB Works!" This workforce initiative involved assembling a range of nonprofits, each serving different ethnic communities coexisting in a specific geographic target area in Long Beach, and treating them as "intake valves" for a community-wide system for identifying, training, and placing residents in jobs.

- **The Northern California Citizenship Project** (NCCP) was formed in May 1997 as a regional regranting and technical assistance project to rapidly mobilize resources to respond to the increased demand for citizenship services. Soon after, the NCCP developed a regional infrastructure for regranting funds, providing technical assistance and training, and supporting more collaborative and effective service delivery at the local level. This first phase of NCCP's activities involved leveraging over $10 million and assisting in the development of a collaborative of seventy agencies in twelve countries to help immigrants through the citizenship process. In January 2000, the NCCP shifted its focus to support efforts that involve newly naturalized citizens and other immigrants in civic life.

- **The Detroit Community Development Funders' Collaborative** was created with the awareness of the importance of community development corporations to their neighborhoods and to the city of Detroit as a whole. It is committed to partnering with those organizations to further the revitalization of Detroit. Established in 1994, the Funders' Collaborative provides financial support and technical assistance to selected community development corporations (CDCs). The Funders' Collaborative raised $11.5 million for its initial five-year program, which provided essential operating and capacity-building support through grants to sixteen CDCs. Capacity building is central to the mission of the Funders' Collaborative. By helping CDCs stabilize operations, install up-to-date accounting and management systems, and build staff depth and expertise, the Funders' Collaborative is playing a critically important role in equipping the organizations to undertake larger and more complex real estate projects. The Funders' Collaborative expects to raise $7.15 million for its second program, a three-year initiative that is part of a joint campaign with the Detroit LISC.

- **The Trenton Funders Collaborative** was formed in Mercer County, New Jersey, when five area foundations came together to address the obstacles facing Trenton public benefit corporations in delivering services. Research confirmed that the most constructive way to help Trenton's nonprofits would be by providing a broad range of technical assistance aimed at improving their management efficiency. The Princeton Area Community Foundation, the Mary Owen Borden Foundation, the Bunbury Company, the Fund for New Jersey, and the Harbourton Foundation collectively committed up to $250,000 a year for three years to establish and run the Technical Assistance Center in Trenton. The Center provides consulting to nonprofit agencies and directs them to specialized services in many areas including finance, human resources, advocacy, fundraising, management, and technology training.

- **The Strategic Alliance Fund** (SAF) began in 1995 as a funder collaborative to promote and support collaboration among nonprofit organizations. Twenty corporate and foundation funders (such as the Ford Foundation, Chase Manhattan Foundation, GE Fund, and the Foundation for Child Development), as well as the United Way of New York City, contributed more than $2 million through SAF. The original purpose was to fund nonprofit collaborations in order to help organizations reduce costs while maintaining service availability at a time of state and city budget cuts. When the financial crisis eased after SAF's first year, the grants were made to promote interdisciplinary, collaborative services for families and youth. The funders, as well as representatives from social service providers, sit on an oversight committee where everyone receives one vote, regardless of their investment in the fund. United Way manages operations for SAF, but the grants are not part of the United Way process. Evaluations of SAF grantees found that many had improved the efficiency of their service delivery or management systems and created new joint programs.

- **The Finance Project**, based in Washington, D.C., was created to fill a void in knowledge about financing issues and strategies related to education, family and children's services, and community building and development, and to put these issues on the national agenda. The Finance Project produces knowledge, tools, technical assistance, and information sources that all funders can use to understand how to finance and sustain policies, programs, and initiatives that improve results for children, families, and communities. It has developed its capacity to understand financing issues across multiple systems and now serves as an intellectual and technical resource to policy makers, program developers, and community leaders. The project was initially started by eleven funders for a three-year period, but is now funded by grants and contacts from federal, state, and local governments; community organizations; collaboratives; and foundations.

- **The David and Lucile Packard, James Irvine, and Flora and William Hewlett Foundations** jointly fund "Strategic Solutions," a five-year initiative conducted by LaPiana Associates to impact the nonprofit sector's perception, understanding, and use of strategic restructuring as part of organizational improvement. Highlighting collaboration and other types of restructuring, the project includes technical assistance, training, and partnerships with both community foundations and intermediary organizations.

- **The Funders' Collaborative for Strong Latino Communities** has raised almost $20 million over three years to strengthen the organizational capacity and infrastructure of the Latino nonprofit sector and to cultivate the next generation of Latino leadership. A subgroup of Hispanics in Philanthropy (HIP), their conviction is that the impressive growth in the Latino population has not been met with a commensurate increase in the level of financial support to Latino-led nonprofit organizations or in the development of leadership in Latino communities. The Funders' Collaborative creates a grantmaking model that increases the amount and the scope of philanthropic support; educates participating funders, HIP members, and nonprofits about issues facing Latino communities; and promotes the development of effective Latino leadership.

- **The Build Initiative** was created by the Early Childhood Funders' Collaborative (ECFC), a consortium of national and local foundations that have substantial grantmaking programs in early childhood care and education. The Collaborative provides networking, information sharing, and strategic grantmaking opportunities to its members. The fifteen ECFC members who have chosen to fund the Build Initiative comprise the Funders' Advisory Council. Five states receive grants to build coordinated, comprehensive early-learning systems. These states, along with four learning partner states, are engaged in a Learning Community to exchange information and ideas on systems building. The foundations hope that private funds will stimulate public investment for durable early learning systemic change. The Council also provides broad strategic oversight of the Initiative.

- **The Philadelphia Neighborhood Development Collaborative** (PNDC) is a collaborative effort of foundations and corporations that is focused on strengthening Philadelphia's community development field. The PNDC does this by providing support to a select group of community development corporations to aid them in achieving significant neighborhood revitalization; advocating for and aggregating additional funds; convening supporters and other stakeholders; and engaging in partnerships with CDCs to plan and implement strategic development initiatives that have the potential to make a significant impact on neighborhood revitalization.

- **The Early Childhood Funders' Collaborative** (ECFC) is an informal association of national, regional, and local foundation representatives with an expressed funding priority in early childhood care and education. The ECFC was established in the early 1990s to improve communications among funders, provide opportunities for mutual learning, identify issues of common concern, incubate ideas for advancing the field, and collaborate on initiatives. The ECFC seeks to promote the interests of children and families, to assist in moving the public forward, and to provide leadership to potential partners in philanthropy, business, and government. Programmatically, the Collaborative relies on three key themes: additional funding is essential to building quality early care and education systems; increasing public and political desire for additional investments is necessary to gain the needed funding; and states are laboratories for change in building and improving early learning systems.

- **The TechFunders Collaborative** is a new and evolving initiative of diverse foundations. Its mission is to collaborate as grantmakers across sectors to advance knowledge, advocate best practices, and fund projects that use information and communication technology (ICT) to strengthen nonprofits. The Collaborative is open to any grantmaker with an interest in technology-related grantmaking. Starting with an inaugural convening in March 2002, funders and strategists have met regularly and have identified three common themes that drive their concerns about technology-related grantmaking. First among these is a sense of urgency around the systemic challenges—including nonprofit adoption, underlying infrastructure, and traditional foundation risk aversion—that are shaping technology-related grantmaking. The second is a thirst for deeper discussions with peers, practitioners, and academic experts on a host of issues associated with technology-related grantmaking. And the third is a desire to engage in initiatives as a group where individual funder effort would have little to no impact.

As impressive as these examples are, they nonetheless represent a tentative trend. These approximately three dozen collaboratives involve, at most, a few hundred foundations and manage only a few hundred million dollars in assets. Most certainly, some funder collaboratives are missing from this list. But to put the numbers in context, the Foundation Center reports that there are 61,800 grantmaking institutions in this country, representing a combined $476 billion in assets and $30.5 billion in annual giving.[3] Funder collaboration currently affects only a miniscule percentage of philanthropic funding streams.

Yet these examples have much to teach. Several of philanthropy's observers have sought to categorize funder collaboratives into taxonomies from which we may identify patterns. Ralph Hamilton, with the Chapin Hall Center for Children, offers that types of funder collaboratives can be arrayed along a spectrum, according to the depth of commitment, from light cooperation to formal foundation consortia. He helpfully groups them according to the tools and mechanics through which they operate, such as democratically managed pooled funds, co-funding arrangements, grant coordination systems, information clearinghouses, and temporary joint ventures.[4] And he analyzes the relative difficulties and merits of these different approaches.

This book, however, is less concerned with operational and organizational distinctions and more concerned with the new behaviors that all funder collaboratives make possible, regardless of their form. And it is focused on the benefits that collaborative participants gain, regardless of the type of collaborative.

Taken collectively, these funder collaboratives serve as a learning laboratory for innovative philanthropic practices, as well as a window into the future of the philanthropy where it is more highly effective in achieving social returns and more comprehensive in its outlook. They conjure up images of funders taking more ambitious, calculated risks and embracing a greater degree of democratization in their work. And they depict a more coherent professional field in which information is shared intelligently and long-term directions are set deliberately.

Each of the remaining chapters in this book will examine one set of behaviors and how and why funder collaboratives foster them. The final chapter will draw some overall conclusions about the cumulative effect of these behaviors, and how we can act deliberately through a range of institutions to translate these experiences from a collection of interesting experiments to a new mode of operation for the entire philanthropic field.

Notes

1. In this chapter, synopses of current funder collaboratives are drawn in part from the excellent research conducted by Ralph Hamilton at the Chapin Hall Center for Children at the University of Chicago, Lucy Bernholz at Blueprint Consulting, and Tom Backer at the Human Interaction Research Institute.
2. Bernholz, Lucy. *The Deliberate Evolution.* (Paper published by Blueprint Research and Design, San Francisco, 2000), 2.
3. Statistics courtesy of the Foundation Center Research Database, February 2003.
4. Hamilton, Ralph. *Moving Ideas and Money: Issues in Funder Collaboration.* (Paper prepared for the Funders' Network for Smart Growth and Livable Communities, Chapin Hall Center for Children, University of Chicago, 2002).

CHAPTER 3

Funder Collaboration as a Tool for Increasing Philanthropic Efficiency

Efficiency is of fundamental concern to grantmakers. Because philanthropic resources are always limited, there are profound opportunity costs associated with any grant decision. While there is likely to be debate among funders about what constitutes efficiency, there is little argument that it should be a primary value behind the way we allocate resources and run our foundations. As a result, foundations are adopting practices that lead to more realistic objective setting, accurate risk assessment, precise outcome measurement, improved capacity to deliver, and higher efficiency of returns on their investments.

But while funders increasingly consider their effectiveness as individual foundations, they rarely discuss the effectiveness of their field as a whole. This question, the topic of this chapter, has to do with assessing the system of working relationships among foundations: It entails pooling knowledge across institutions; facilitating the formation of groupings, networks, or alliances to do things collectively; reducing duplication of effort; and optimizing collective economies of scale.

This chapter will explore some ways that collaborative grantmaking can result in greater philanthropic efficiencies than could ever be achieved through individual donor action. And it will also consider how a more efficient philanthropic field in turn can increase the efficiency of individual foundations.

Investments of General Value

One way for a group of funders to think about achieving economies of scale is to pool funds to cover program expenses that they all face in common. Especially in the case of large, multilayered initiatives, there are often investments to be made that would increase the efficiency of everyone's grantmaking but would be inefficient for any one foundation to take on alone.

For example, many of the front-end expenses involved in mounting a neighborhood initiative fall into this category. There are now, or have been, numerous funder collaboratives that have coalesced around major initiatives in geographic areas of concentrated poverty: the Detroit Funders Collaborative, the Philadelphia Neighborhood Development Collaborative, the Baltimore Neighborhood Collaborative, the Trenton Funders Collaborative, the East Bay Funders, the Los Angeles Urban Funders (LAUF), the Long Beach Funders, and the San Diego Neighborhood Funders, to name a few.

Activities commonly carried out by these collaboratives include preliminary research, resident canvassing, mapping of local nonprofits, communitywide strategic planning, and the facilitation of local groups into networks or alliances around outcomes. All of these activities benefit each funder making grants in the community. They ensure that the nonprofits they support will be part of a larger, communitywide effort and in doing so, achieve leverage.

Rather than one funder assuming the entire burden of underwriting these activities, or having multiple funders duplicate the effort, it is more efficient for the funders to pool resources and share the costs as a group. At Long Beach Funders, Julie Meenan, the head of a local family foundation, recalls the excitement of investing $300,000 in front-end consulting dollars to develop the model for their workforce initiative: "We had never used consultants, and having access to these experts was euphoric. It was something most of us would not have done alone."

In one of its target communities, the Los Angeles Urban Funders (LAUF) made a set of investments aimed at strengthening a network of school-based parent centers as a platform for resident engagement and service delivery for a neighborhood-wide initiative. These included the material costs of setting up and furnishing an unused classroom in each school to serve as a parent center; the staffing of these centers with trained parents; the development of an annual needs survey among parents; and management classes designed to build productive working relations between parent center staff and school administrators.

Few foundations would have considered it an efficient use of their funds to support activities such as these, especially since they yielded few concrete outcomes. But once these centers were up and running, they served as an infrastructure for the effective delivery of a wide range of programs: They presented an instant mechanism for recruiting thousands of parents as clients for services; they provided comfortable, familiar locations to hold self-help meetings, English classes, or counseling sessions; and they became one-stop centers for information and assistance.

At one point or another, every LAUF member foundation utilized the parent centers. Health conversion foundations found them to be an effective way to reach large numbers of local residents with information about medical screenings or free health insurance programs. Education funders found them to be ideal for administering adult literacy classes or workshops for parents wishing to help their children attend college. These parent centers became the staging ground for the development and operation of community arts projects, extracurricular athletic programs, employment strategies, domestic abuse workshops, parenting classes, and more.

Another example of funders sharing the cost of generalizable investments is the Southern Funders Collaborative. This group of funders, in partnership with the Southern Partners Fund, the Appalachian Community Fund, and the Fund for Southern Communities, created a pool of funding to enhance the overall capacity of nonprofit groups throughout the South. Each grantee organization received an operating grant as well as technical assistance funding that could be used to seek help for a specific organizational issue or challenge.

These investments have helped to improve the state of the nonprofit infrastructure in the South, rendering it a more effective apparatus for carrying out community-based work and a more fertile ground for philanthropic investment. The Collaborative initiates a new round of grants and technical assistance awards each year, strengthening new sets of key nonprofits.

Shared Staff

A second area where collaboration can generate efficiencies is shared staffing. Neighborhood-based collaboratives again provide an excellent example. Funders quickly recognize that it will take more resources, time, and their own effort to participate in large-scale neighborhood initiatives than in anything they have done before. Their diverse efforts, concentrated in the same geographic areas, could easily become redundant or send conflicting signals to local groups. Shared staff can reduce duplication, pool expertise, and minimize costs.

These shared staff persons often have a different profile from the average program officer. To assemble all the information necessary for complex funding decisions, such staff often need to consult with a wide range of experts, specialists, outside vendors, and site visitors. They will typically consult with more people and make more visits during the grantee investigation and implementation periods than the average program officer. In fact, the initiative being undertaken may be so complex that no one person will possess the mix of talents and skills necessary to get the job done. A diverse team of consultants may be a better fit.

These shared staff persons, removed from traditional expectations, are often freer to be more proactive than the average program officer. Instead of conducting reviews of proposals received, this individual or individuals will often work with applicants to shape their proposals into something representing communitywide interest. They require an ability to envision collaborative organizational structures that no one agency would likely think of on its own. If they exert too much influence in formulating the solution, they run the risk of being seen as manipulative. The individual should therefore have firm values and a moral barometer. This staff must not merely negotiate between two sides, but needs to create spaces, events, and learning opportunities within which all stakeholders can find winning solutions.

A strong example of the benefits of shared staff is the Northern California Citizenship Project (NCCP). It was formed as a regional regranting and technical assistance project in response to the immigration provisions of the 1997 Federal Welfare Reform Act. In order to rapidly mobilize resources to respond to the increased demand for citizenship services, the NCCP developed a highly effective regional infrastructure to regrant funds, provide technical assistance and training, and support collaboration and effective service delivery at the local level. Far from acting solely as a regranting body, the NCCP engaged in a wide variety of regional activities that supported and expanded on local efforts. It was important that such efforts be staffed in a centralized way and that funders not build redundant systems. The primary staff person also needed to be free to bring different constituencies together.

A counterargument to shared staffing plans is that they represent an unnecessary set of employees to be paid—and add another wasteful level to the nonprofit infrastructure. Robert Sherman at the Funders' Collaborative on Youth Organizing (FCYO) submits that if the collaborative's staff are usefully employed in roles that add to the value of the group, then it should not be second-guessed. "The money would only be poorly spent if the staff were doing the same old thing."

Increasing Overall Nonprofit Effectiveness

Sometimes, in order for all foundations to maximize their effectiveness, there needs to be a complete restructuring of the system of nonprofits in that community. This might involve a redivision of responsibilities among the nonprofits, mergers and acquisitions, or the formation of networks or referral relationships. Arguably, the most impressive large-scale illustration of a funder collaborative using its resources to support system-wide restructuring among nonprofits is the Minnesota Futures Fund.

The Minnesota Futures Fund was a response to the federal budget cuts and the devolution of responsibility for many federal programs to state and local governments. These trends threatened the safety net for thousands of vulnerable individuals and families in Minnesota, and the local nonprofits were faced with the overwhelming task of picking up the slack in a time of reduced resources. It was clear to local funders that business as usual would not suffice and that they needed to pool their resources and invest them in ways that would help the entire nonprofit infrastructure function more effectively. Nonprofit leaders needed the financial freedom to explore totally new approaches to service delivery.

The Fund was created through the commitment of three statewide membership organizations—the Minnesota Council on Foundations, the Minnesota Council of Nonprofits, and the Minnesota Council of Churches, as well as thirty-nine grantmakers and the state of Minnesota. Together they amassed a $2 million pooled fund that nonprofits could access in order to jointly undertake comprehensive planning and systems analysis.

These funds were used for a variety of purposes. Some agencies revised their mission statements and restructured their operations and staffing patterns. New relationships were created between and among these agencies in order to better assist individuals and families in addressing the wide array of barriers facing them as they left welfare rolls. Lightweight and flexible networks were created to coordinate service referrals and ensure that no client would fall through the cracks. Many clients were directly involved in the planning. Duplication of services was minimized, resources were conserved, and shared evaluation systems were put in place.

According to the evaluation report released in 1999, this massive planning and coordination process resulted in immediate and direct benefits to clients. Individual agencies were reporting a reduction in the prolonged use of homeless shelters, better access and utilization of healthcare and transportation programs, and increases in workplace readiness skills. Because of the overall systems reforms, each individual agency was better equipped to serve its clients.

There are other examples of how funder collaboration can produce the complete dismantling and restructuring of nonprofit infrastructure. In 1995, the Early Childhood Funders' Collaborative, a consortium of national and local foundations, was established to share information about successful program and policy interventions in early childhood education and to identify opportunities for strategic partnerships. Participants included the Caroline and Sigmund Schott Foundation, the George Gund Foundation, the Lucent Technologies Foundation, the Harris Foundation, the Ewing Marion Kauffman Foundation, the McKnight Foundation, the A. L. Mailman Family Foundation, the W. K. Kellogg Foundation, the Robert R. McCormick Tribune Foundation, the Schumann Fund for New Jersey, and the David and Lucile Packard Foundation.

Among the strategic partnerships emerging from this collaborative is the Build Initiative, a multi-state partnership designed to help states create a streamlined continuum of programs and services that develop children from birth through age five. The Initiative was inspired by recent research showing that children do much of their most important learning in their first years. Early childhood partnerships in four states—Illinois, Minnesota, New Jersey, and Ohio—have been chosen to receive initial two-year awards based on a range of criteria, including their readiness to build comprehensive systems of early care and education. Partnership teams including state agency officials, business and community leaders, parents, advocates, and others will develop state-specific strategies to help ensure the healthy development of young children.

Reduced Duplication

In any community, there is a need for many different kinds of funding to be allocated to where they are needed most. It is important that one issue area, such as education, not have more funding than it requires, while another—let's say, environmental issues—does not have enough. What is needed is a mechanism through which funding streams are directed and coordinated so as to avoid "floods" and "droughts."

In a way, funder collaboratives can serve as a framework within which individual foundations can better understand the interdependence of different types of foundation grants and how they can reinforce one another's work. In its ideal state, this system of funding streams would function as what Joseph Galaskiewicz[1] calls a "grants economy" through which highly decentralized grantmaking decisions would be rationalized, creating a "network for collective action." Like the marketplace, it could aggregate many individual voluntary decisions in order to better allocate resources. And like government, it could produce public goods and broad societal improvements.

To function like a "grants economy," donors need to have specializations and market niches negotiated among themselves and professional associations, and an efficient marketplace based on good communication. Funder collaboratives, by consolidating the management of multiple diverse funding streams, are a natural place to take a systemic look at philanthropy as a financial market for nonprofits. They are microcosms within which we can explore ways of creating more predictable funding streams and efficient capital flows to nonprofits. As such, collaboratives also present opportunities to model more rational systems for philanthropic investments.

An excellent example in the field of arts is found in the Los Angeles Arts Funders. The coordinator of this group conducted simple surveys of every known arts funder in the county—collecting data on the size, term, and purpose of every grant—and aggregated the results. She concluded that there was a preponderance of funding for studio arts, for example, but a shortage in the area of dance. Information like this has allowed arts funders in Southern California, for the first time, to plan for more efficient distribution of funds.

Addressing Nonprofit Inefficiencies

Inadvertently, philanthropy is at the cause of many inefficiencies at the community level. From the grantee perspective, there is the baffling array of sources nonprofits typically face in their search for support, the diverse proposals that need to be prepared, and the tangle of different funding cycles and timelines that must be reconciled in order to maintain a steady flow of support for their activities. In the midst of this confusion, grantees generally bear the full cost of and extensive time associated with proposal writing and presentation, while confronting unknown and uncertain odds of actually receiving the grant.

By collectively mapping their various funding streams, it was possible for LAUF members to discern, for the first time, overall funding patterns in the neighborhood. They were able to gain a sense of the dollar sums of public and private resources, the duration of support, and the purposes assigned to this funding. They were able to draw conclusions about what program areas were underfunded (or overfunded) and how they could fill the gaps. Individual funders were able to see their giving in the larger ecology of funding sources and determine how theirs could be spent most effectively. And to a limited extent, at least, they were able to present this information in a rational, organized way to nonprofits.

Russell Sakaguchi, as executive director of the ARCO Foundation, put it this way. "If organizations in the LAUF target areas could predict and plan for the funding coming into the community (according to source, purposes, access points, duration, etc.), this would enable these groups to mount long-term strategies. This information would help them to figure out much bigger questions and help the neighborhoods to set their goals."

The process is even harder for nonprofits attempting to create more efficient inter-agency partnerships and collaborative structures. Funders tend to view non-profits as isolated enterprises and set up competition among them for scarce resources. Extremely few funding sources are made available expressly for the purposes of establishing and maintaining a nonprofit collaboration.

In response, LAUF set aside the pooled fund to be used as a counterbalance to these dynamics. These monies could be used to finance collaborative efforts across nonprofits and other community stakeholders. LAUF staff also participated directly by convening and facilitating the partners. By assuming direct responsibility for the construction and maintenance of a major neighborhood initiative involving many partners, LAUF members quickly began to observe how philanthropy can sometimes fail to provide the financial instruments that would be most useful. They could clearly observe that large-scale initiatives and neighborhood collaboratives require an efficient capital market where resources have few restrictions and flow readily to where they are needed.

As a result of this analysis, LAUF made its staff available to absorb some of the work of collaborative proposal development associated with the initiative. During the entire process of designing and installing the workforce initiative in Pacoima, LAUF staff not only helped to craft the workplan but played an intermediating role helping to manage the funding, monitor performance, and prepare reports so that the executive director could focus on the many immediate demands of developing a new program. Some have suggested that the workforce initiative succeeded in large part because its director was not preoccupied with fundraising.

As described earlier, restricted grants to specific organizations still play an important role in financing such initiatives. Each LAUF funder gives grants to specific agencies that correspond with their funding priorities. Just as individual foundations speak of their "grants portfolio," LAUF assembles a portfolio of grants from across the foundations. In some ways, these grants are quite traditional gifts to ordinary nonprofits for categorical activities. The difference is that funders are expected to have a logic model for how these grantees feed into the initiative, contributing to the overall community outcome.

Short-Term Efficiencies

Although it may seem counterintuitive to think of a group of funders acting more quickly than a solitary foundation, that is sometimes the case. When emergencies arise, funders are often willing to make exceptions, removing resources from restrictions and pooling them in one place for greater accessibility to grantees. Funder collaboratives have formed around unexpected government funding cuts, natural disasters, and acts of war or terrorism.

There was a proliferation of short-term funder collaboratives, eager to move resources as efficiently as possible, in the days after September 11, 2001. A prime example of a funder collaborative's expediency is the New York Arts Recovery Fund, spearheaded by the New York Foundation for the Arts. After September 11, the already undercapitalized arts community in New York struggled to survive. There are more than two hundred arts organizations—and thousands of individual artists—located below 14th Street who were in need of an immediate infusion of financial support.

The New York Arts Recovery Fund, seeded by the Rockefeller Foundation and the Robert Sterling Clark Foundation, made available a rapid emergency grant program in collaboration with the nonprofit Finance Fund and Artist Community Federal Credit Union. The Fund also supported on-the-ground distribution of information on alternative funding sources and helped to advocate on a grassroots level for a fair share of public aid monies. A large foundation would have likely had a difficult time navigating so effectively in such a localized area and within such a compressed time frame.

Long-Term Efficiencies

One of the greatest inefficiencies in philanthropy is the tendency of funders to support an effort for two or three years and then move on to another grantee. They frequently seed pilot projects but rarely stick with them long enough to help them achieve their potential. This is extremely inefficient in that startup costs are recreated every few years and nonprofits must invest tremendous time and labor in the cultivation of new contributions.

Again, funder collaboratives offer a remedy. The fact that a pooled fund can remain in place as a continuing, uninterrupted funding stream—even as individual contributors may come and go—provides a measure of stability that is rarely found otherwise. By creating continuity, collaboratives are often able to build on successes from year to year. They help nonprofit executives to bypass the inefficiencies of random hit-or-miss fundraising so that they can dedicate more time to their programmatic work.

Temporary Efficiencies: Sustainability Planning

In terms of sustainability, funder collaboratives help major initiatives transition into sustainability more readily because they represent an in-place collection of diverse donors. Many large foundations have taken on major initiatives by themselves, absorbing all costs. When the time comes for the foundations to step back from supporting the initiative, they often look for other funders to pick up the costs, a daunting challenge. But when the original initiative is funded by a group of foundations, there is a ready-and-waiting group of potential funders to take on all or portions of the continued work.

In this sense, it may very well be that the collaborative structure provides certain efficiencies for a period of time, but that it should not be a permanent entity. Often, the high-risk efforts will become less risky over time. At that point, individual donors can and should take on funding responsibilities. In this sense, the function of the funder collaborative is to put in place major initiatives and then, once they are fully stabilized efforts, hand them off to individual foundations to be funded through more routine funding procedures.

Ironically, funders often cite "inefficiency" as a reason they refrain from joining funder collaboratives. One funder, echoing the concerns of her peers, has asked, "Why should we create yet another level of bureaucracy between our funds and the grantees who need them?" But these collaboratives present a very different picture.

Notes

1. Galaskiewicz, Joseph. *Social Organization of an Urban Grants Economy.* (Orlando: Academic Press, 1985), 209-211.

CHAPTER 4

Funder Collaboration as a Way to Frame Comprehensive Solutions

Societal problems, of the kind typically addressed by private foundations, are usually so complex that no organization can hope to resolve them alone. A panoramic array of interventions is required, as well as a corresponding array of funding streams, to support these interventions. Such challenges require the integration of multiple disciplines, knowledge bases, and intelligences. But philanthropy has borrowed much of its professional approach—not to mention its personnel—from academia, where specializations reign and true generalists are uncommon.

This is not to minimize the importance of narrow areas of expertise. Only foundations that specialize, say, in public health issues, are likely to possess the experience and informed judgment to make wise funding decisions when it comes to health clinics, hospital outreach programs, or preventive health campaigns. Similarly, only a foundation that has focused for years on organized sports programs is likely to understand the challenges of setting up extracurricular athletic leagues or to understand the relative merits of basketball or gymnastics on a child's development.

But there are precious few mechanisms for creatively combining health strategies, athletic programs, or any of the other myriad solutions to social problems. More often than not, they remain isolated, scattershot, and disconnected. A funder collaborative can be a logical way to assemble such diverse perspectives and funding streams, organizing them toward common objectives. The collaborative can support this process in multiple ways.

First, the funder collaborative can serve as a repository of knowledge, collecting from across disciplines and over long periods of time. Amassing this knowledge allows for its maximal utilization. For time-limited purposes, the funder collaborative becomes a giant virtual institution, at times functioning like a single foundation, with numerous distinct but highly integrated departments. Each foundation makes its own independent grants, but they are shaped by the overall initiative and planned as part of a larger portfolio of funding decisions.

Usually, the individual grants remain subject to the internal timelines, criteria, and decision-making procedures of the individual member foundations. But they are nonetheless part and parcel of the whole. As Robert Sherman of the Surdna Foundation explains, "When groups of grantmakers take up a set of questions together, it is not just an individual funder question. The process forces the group to frame questions in a circumspect way that leads to action for all of them." Claire Peeps, executive director of the Durfee Foundation and a member of LAUF, maintains that collaboratives help to ensure a "balanced diet of funding" for large initiatives, with a blend of resources from "every necessary food group."

The richest examples of this observation are found in funder collaboratives created to support major neighborhood initiatives in disinvested urban communities. Communities, by their very nature, are holistic organisms that can only be understood—and acted upon—in a holistic fashion. The comprehensiveness of the knowledge base allows funders to look at the complex interrelationships and interdependencies of the availability of affordable housing, healthcare, commercial development, educational facilities, incidence of crime, and recreational amenities. In a real sense, the initiatives became a shared narrative, a framework within which each foundation learns how its categorical funding stream could fit into a larger enterprise and how to define its giving in relation to other foundations.

Members of Long Beach Funders recall their original daylong planning process as one of the most useful and well-structured aspects of the collaboration. It involved a level of analysis and comprehensive planning that would not have taken place otherwise, and that utilized their collective perspectives. The group analyzed statistics for numerous geographic areas within Long Beach, and ultimately selected 90806 as the target area for their initiative. "It was a definite gain for me to think about funding by zip code," explains Julie Meenan, because it was possible to examine how citywide political and economic trends are localized, and to map the local nonprofit infrastructure. The group was able to analyze how their collective resources could be blended with other funding streams and to consider their capacity to make a difference in the full range of social issues, like homelessness, healthcare, affordable housing, education, and employment.

In the Pacoima neighborhood of Los Angeles, one of the geographic communities designated as a LAUF site, residents and community groups had coalesced around the objective of measurably improving student achievement levels. Focus groups and communitywide parent surveys had suggested that reaching that objective would involve an array of interventions that included classroom reforms, after-school programs, family support services, and an employment strategy for parents.

Within this framework, individual funders could not only make grants to nonprofits working within their issue area, but they could understand how their grantmaking contributed to a wider community outcome. The Los Angeles Amateur

Athletic Foundation, for example, financed three separate extracurricular sports programs for students in this neighborhood and was able to draw empirical conclusions about the correlation between children's participation in sports and their academic performance. Similarly, a funder with an interest in workforce development could trace the connections between parents with secure jobs and the attendance, grades, and conduct of their children.

In some cases, discovering these connections led to whole new programmatic strategies that, in all likelihood, never would have evolved without the existence of the LAUF collaborative. For instance, a program called "Healthy Generations," through which parents were trained to educate their peers about basic public health issues, was connected with the workforce strategy in such a way that parents who had served for a year as paraprofessional health educators were channeled into job opportunities at local hospitals and medical centers. In another health-related example, a school-based dental clinic was conceived, not only as a way to improve family health, but as a teaching opportunity for young children, as an employment opportunity for parents interested in being dental assistants, and as a pipeline for guiding local high school seniors to a prestigious university dental school located nearby.

In two other neighborhoods, Vermont/Manchester and Hyde Park, LAUF has been supporting a substance abuse reduction strategy that is achieving its outcomes through a comprehensive array of interventions that address the four major root causes of addiction: economic marginalization, low educational attainment, inadequate social services, and a proliferation of nuisance properties. By effectively organizing a mix of funding streams that can finance all of these interventions at once, the effort has succeeded in achieving measurable results. And only by carefully tracking and correlating outcomes can funders draw informed conclusions about what worked and what didn't.

In those communities, there are now member foundations simultaneously supporting the following strategies within the target area: group homes for young mothers struggling with addiction; mental health counseling for individuals with histories of drug abuse; twelve-step programs for individuals fighting addiction; a transitional program for individuals recently released from prison; and a local pressure campaign aimed at increasing public funding for all of these programs. On the preemptive side, there are job placement agencies assisting individuals in avoiding substance abuse by finding decent employment and mentors helping high school students stay off the streets and go to college. Organized resident groups are fighting for the removal of liquor stores and motels that serve as outlets for drugs and alcohol in the community.

In each of these neighborhoods, the funding mix was not comprehensive merely in terms of categorical funding areas represented, but it was also diverse in terms of the array of financial instruments used. Every major neighborhood initiative will require money in many different forms, sums, terms, and durations. It will at one time or another require seed grants for resident groups, startup grants for new organizations, stabilization grants for groups in trouble, program grants for specific activities, core operating support for key agencies, and planning grants for collaborative efforts. LAUF members have gained a greater appreciation of the interdependence of these different types of funding and how they can reinforce one another. Unexpected consequences have included a variety of new working relationships among LAUF member institutions outside of the LAUF context: joint funding agreements, grantee referrals, regranting arrangements, and new funder collaboratives.

Geography at any level can provide a context for comprehensive philanthropic strategies. In the same way that neighborhoods can be treated as the units for common action, regions can also serve to organize funder efforts. In the Great Lakes region, for example, the John D. and Catherine T. MacArthur Foundation began convening four other Chicago-area funders for monthly lunch meetings on regional topics. Each of the five foundations was historically invested in the Great Lakes region and had an extensive portfolio of grants within it. Together, they conducted educational forums through their regional association of grantmakers. They also jointly funded large-scale projects representing multiple facets of regional development, including affordable housing, transportation planning, and environmental resource management. More recently, the group has launched a series of interviews with key nonprofit leaders in the area to ascertain how these regional initiatives can be sustained.

To be truly comprehensive, region-based funder collaboratives need to integrate both the physical and human dimensions of development. In Michigan, the Charles Stewart Mott Foundation is coordinating a planning effort that combines both land use and human development perspectives. Program officers from the Mott Foundation have convened and networked a variety of Michigan funders to carry out a comprehensive assessment of environmental and racial equality indicators in the region. Working collaboratively with nonprofits and public entities, the funders are framing the results of this research as a blueprint for holistic action.

Place-based funder collaboratives are not the only examples of funder collaboratives promoting comprehensive solutions. Funders for Sustainable Food Systems (FSFS), a funder collaborative based in San Francisco, demonstrates a different approach: the bringing together of different categorical specializations to create a multidisciplinary brain trust capable of breakthrough thinking. The FSFS holds a vision of California as the leader and model state in the development of sustainable food systems. But instead of realizing that vision through the creation of new, dedicated funding sources, FSFS reorients and redirects an array of existing funding streams.

The FSFS promotes its vision to a great many funders, raising their awareness of the critical need for, and multiple problem areas addressed by, sustainable food systems. Areas such as public health, environmental degradation, labor rights, marine ecosystems, animal welfare, and food security are innately linked to the way food is grown, distributed, and consumed in California. The premise is that if foundations working in each of these areas were to understand how their grantmaking can contribute—either directly or indirectly—to the creation of a sustainable food system, they could adjust the type of grants they make accordingly. Toward this end, FSFS convenes grantmakers from various sectors as a forum to work together and identify opportunities for systemic solutions.

In another example, the Consultative Group on Biological Diversity (CGBD) brings together a range of environmental funders into one network. In doing so, it becomes possible for funders to make better decisions that take into account the perspective of many environmental constituencies and interest groups. Out of this diverse affinity group, smaller working groups form to tackle concrete projects in specific areas such as marine science, coastal habitats, and rain forests. Individual funders are not recruited into these working groups but self-organize based on their self-interests. The CGBD provides organizational support, a secretariat, and coordination for the group.

The Sustainable Forestry Funders is one such working group that has emerged in the context of the CGBD. It aims to both expand foundation understanding of issues around sustainable forestry and certification and to provide a venue for strategic discussion and collaboration. Originally an independent affiliation of funders staffed primarily through the offices of the Rockefeller Brothers Fund, the Sustainable Forestry Funders is now a formally recognized subgroup of the CGBD Forests Working Group.

Yet another way of achieving comprehensiveness is to create large, unrestricted pooled funds that can be used without deference to program guidelines. In a way, this is the ultimate dissolution of categories in favor of comprehensiveness. An excellent example of this approach can be found in the Racial Justice Collaborative. The Racial Justice Collaborative was built around the observation that the civil rights movement, while effectively dismantling legal segregation, left much more work to be done. Blatant discrimination on the basis of race, color, ethnicity, national origin, and language persists, or resurfaces in new forms. New discriminatory laws have arisen in the last decade in response to a burgeoning Latin American immigration population. Other forms of legal discrimination have been enacted in response to domestic security concerns. For members of the Racial Justice Collaborative, these injustices demand the kind of resistance and reform witnessed during the 1960s.

Equally troubling are the more structural forms of exclusion, the nonlegal vestiges of earlier discrimination against African-Americans or the inequities that African-Americans have inherited from generations of exclusion. Other structural forms of exclusion include the widespread beliefs and biases that, while not manifested as explicit discriminatory laws, nevertheless permeate the way public resources are allocated, services are delivered, or private sector markets are defined. For these more pervasive and insidious forms of exclusion, the frontal assault normally waged by lawyers will not work. What is required instead is a comprehensive set of strategies carried out in every arena of social life—healthcare, education, economic development, business, etc.—that incorporates both the insights of lawyers and the grassroots human relationships of community-based organizations.

The Racial Justice Collaborative has a pooled fund intended to support part-nerships between lawyers and local community-based organizations working in areas of racial justice. Although the Collaborative defines its work in legal terms, it seeks opportunities to fund "lawyering" approaches in the broadest possible sense. These include strategies that aim to address the range of contributing factors to racial injustice. Resources have been used by local partnerships to take action in the areas of education, healthcare access, immigration and citizenship, labor issues, voter rights, and economic justice.

The purpose of the Collaborative's pooled fund is to provide multiyear, flexible funding that will enable organizations to strengthen partnerships around racial justice community work. Support is intended to build organizational experience with creative legal approaches and permit the creation of collaborative networks and sophisticated problem-solving and communication strategies. To this end, the fund supports training, knowledge development, infrastructure development, and relationship building—especially relationship building between community activists and lawyers.

The fund also supports activities that are integral to an innovative approach to racial justice but for which funding is often difficult to secure: for example, the plan-ning and coordination of community meetings; preparation of community members to engage in discussion with local agencies; provision of translation and interpreta-tion services; public education campaigns and other communication approaches; production and distribution of informational materials; purchase of advertisements in local and ethnic media; production, translation, and distribution of informational videos, CDs or other media; participatory research on community claims/legal issues; preparation and dissemination of policy data; staff time of lawyers and com-munity activists needed to interface with each other and support one another's work; technological assistance and technology that supports constituency building; office space for prolonged local campaigns; and staff time for negotiation with government agencies.

————————

What all of these funder collaboratives accomplish is the melding of the categorical silos that can limit philanthropy's effectiveness without sacrificing the benefits of these specializations. They do this either by literally declassifying and pooling the funds—and turning them over to a multidisciplinary funding body—or by setting up the systems required to coordinate and align diverse funding streams. And in the best examples, they blend the various human resources in the collaborative to create hyperintelligence.

By themselves, these collaboratives do not promote comprehensiveness outside the context of their own work; the effect is limited to the specific initiatives that they support or to the confines of their structured conversations. They do not, as individual efforts, transform philanthropy.

But they expand the horizons of the funders who participate in transformative ways. Many participants suggest that the way they define the scope of their categorical funding area has been permanently expanded as a result of their participation in comprehensive collaboratives. They know that when a particular problem calls for comprehensive solutions, they have at their disposal a means to respond.

CHAPTER 5

Funder Collaboratives as Vehicles for Fostering Risk Taking

If foundations only supported projects with easily measured short-term outcomes, there would be few ambitious efforts to improve society. Breakthrough social innovations, by their very nature, require the acceptance of risk. And even in the case of failures, philanthropy stands to learn important lessons that result from its high-risk work, thereby enhancing the prospects for success over time.

But while risk is important to effective philanthropy, it is in short supply. With their origins in legacies, wills, and endowments, private foundations often value tradition, history, and a sense of the past. Corporate foundations, more often than not, view their charitable contributions conservatively—as insurance policies that will protect their parent companies from negative publicity. In short, although there are extremely few real constraints on philanthropy's ability to take risks, donors tend to circumscribe their work before they even begin.

This chapter will consider whether a funder collaborative is an effective way to promote deliberate risk-taking and nontraditional behaviors among grantmakers, and whether risks taken in the context of a funder collaborative can affect ongoing practices in individual foundations. More specifically, this chapter will look at some nonconventional strategies that have evolved in the context of funder collaboratives and analyze why they were able to arise. It will also consider whether these risky strategies could ever spread beyond the rarified "hothouse" atmosphere of the collaborative to permeate participating institutions or the wider field.

How Real Is Philanthropic Risk?

There is little evidence that foundations face any negative consequences for risks they may take. There are few, if any, foundations that are widely regarded as institutional failures and few practices that would draw the attention of regulatory agencies. Among individual grantmakers, it is hard to think of specific colleagues who have been publicly ridiculed, labeled incompetent, or sanctioned for taking risks.

Nevertheless, philanthropy is decidedly risk averse. Maybe funders are less concerned with failing to deliver on their mission than with choosing a mission that is regarded as unpopular or controversial in the first place. Perhaps they are preoccupied with stretching the legal limits prescribed by tax laws and attracting federal regulations. It might even be simply that funders are paralyzed by opportunity costs, worried that a risky strategy could divert precious resources from a more surefire success.

Or perhaps the problem lies not in a fear of risk at all, but in a simple lack of *incentives* to take risks. There is no bundle of rewards to promote risk taking—no public accolades or increased compensation for risks that pay off. The organizational structures and group norms that make risk desirable in other fields are absent in the foundation world. All of philanthropy's infrastructure organizations are membership associations, and membership associations, with the possible exception of trade unions, inherently share a low threshold for risk. This is because they generally seek to move only in directions supported by the majority of their members.

What's more, funders know that any lessons they might learn from failed risks would probably be of no value to other funders. There is little evidence that funders are interested in sharing their learnings with one another. This is, in part, because foundations and nonprofits collect little solid data on their work, and so there are few meaningful conclusions that can be drawn from program experiences. Even where reliable data exist, many funders refrain from discussing their failures because of the perceived harm to the grantees. After all, the consequences for the grantee—discontinuation of funds, disappointed constituents or communities, and injured reputation—are much more significant than for the grantmaker.

How Does a Funder Collaborative Foster Risk Taking?

In large part, collaboratives make risk taking easier simply because responsibility—and by extension, the cost of failures—is dispersed.

A prime example is the Community Financial Resource Center (CFRC), a nonprofit that provides small business assistance, home-buying classes, consumer credit counseling, and subsidized microlending programs in South Los Angeles. In 1992, Los Angeles banks received a dismal assessment of their community reinvestment activities. As a group, they were neglecting South Los Angeles populations as a customer base. Leaders of Southern California's financial services industry, while acknowledging the importance of increasing access to economic opportunities in these areas, complained that the risk was too great: default rates were high and bank branches historically underperformed there.

In response, thirty-nine banks, primarily represented through their corporate foundations, came together to form a collaborative with the city of Los Angeles. They concluded that although a solitary bank might find it too risky to begin developing a market in South Los Angeles, a collaborative of banks could share the expense of building that market. They co-funded the creation of CFRC, which opened its doors in 1993. The CFRC has served over 50,000 residents and business owners, held more than 350 workshops, and developed a range of successful programs. Although bank foundations are often distinct from their corporate parents, participating banks have all gained new customers as a result of these investments.

Another way that funder collaboratives facilitate risk taking is by pooling assets in intermediaries, effectively insulating the funds from the accountability structure of their institutions. For example, the money contributed to the Foundation Consortium for California's Children and Youth was pooled in a fund at the Consortium's independent nonprofit. In this way, the funding was removed from the normal restrictions of the seventeen individual foundations and held in a neutral intermediary where it would be accessible for highly nontraditional usages. This was necessary, the members maintained, because traditional grants to school-linked programs or after-school tutoring centers were insufficient to affect the fate of children across the state in meaningful ways.

Instead, what was required were massive systems reforms: a statewide infrastructure for school-linked services; an integrated strategy for the delivery and monitoring of after-school programs; the alignment of family support and educational programs with statewide standards; and a total redesign of the child welfare system. To accomplish these overwhelming tasks, the Foundation Consortium's resources alone were woefully insufficient. These funds needed to be used as highly strategic investments that would leverage the more massive capital flows of the market or the public sector. Consequently, rather than regranting funds to individual local programs, the Foundation Consortium partnered with government agencies, injecting small amounts of flexible capital into the public systems to support innovations that could be brought to scale. The Foundation Consortium also contracted directly with the private sector in order to mobilize the specific technical assistance and advocacy activities that they knew were needed.

Such investments were considered risky by many or most of the member foundations. Pouring money into a public bureaucracy would have been the height of lunacy to some of their trustees. After all, isn't that what tax dollars are for? And since the government is accountable only to voters (and not to foundations, as nonprofits are), then there was never a guarantee that a particular reform or project would stick. Spending money in the private sector seemed equally foolhardy and potentially explosive. What would people think if they were to learn that foundation dollars were being channeled to private contractors? And what if a particular advocacy issue exploded as a controversial subject of public debate? Would the individual funders be dragged through the press as fomenters of political unrest?

From the perspective of Bonnie Armstrong, a staff person at the Foundation Consortium, anxiety was minimized by the "arm's length" between the contributing foundations and the Consortium itself. If the Consortium succeeded in its work, then the member foundations could rightly boast that they were members of the team that made the bold and risky decisions. And if the efforts failed, the foundation representatives could—again, accurately—explain that the Consortium was a freestanding entity with a board that is separate from the boards of the member foundations.

Despite philanthropy's potential for influencing private market forces and public policy, these have represented two of the most significant areas of perceived risks, since many foundation boards fear drawing the attention of these powerful sectors. The Funders' Network for Smart Growth and Livable Communities has begun to serve as an effective vehicle for groups of foundations wishing to influence the patterns of real estate development or to influence the overall voting tendencies of suburban populations. The Funders' Network is exploring how philanthropy can persuade large-scale real estate syndicates to include "smart growth products" in their product portfolios and to make them readily available to their institutional customers. To make these products feasible, the Funders' Network is prepared to invest financial, human, and intellectual capital in the product development process.

Taking a stand in opposition to a government can be bracing, but also discon-certing. Funder collaboratives have funded efforts that contradict public policies, or step out in front of public leaders with boldness. In 1991, when the AIDS epidemic had reached crisis proportions, but the federal government had still not dedicated sufficient funds to the problem, the Robert Wood Johnson Foundation led the way.

A study on sexual behavior, considered by doctors and epidemiologists to be a critical step in halting the spread of AIDS, had been slated for federal funding, but political controversy had kept those funds from flowing. The Robert Wood Johnson Foundation took the initiative to fund the study, and were then joined by Ford, Rockefeller, MacArthur, Mellon, and Kaiser. As Stephen Isaacs and John Rogers have noted, there was "security in numbers." In the absence of the collaborative structure, some or all of these foundations might have delayed investing in studies like this one, which paved the way for today's most effective AIDS prevention educational campaigns.

At LAUF, funders discovered that they could take greater risks through the col-laborative than they could have ever taken at their own foundations. The individuals representing each foundation were effectively preauthorized to allocate the funds as they saw fit, based on their firsthand interaction with neighborhood leaders in the initiative's three target areas. In a sense, the funding had become a donor-advised fund and the LAUF members were the functional donors. When empowered to act freely, they took on entrepreneurial risks and tested nontraditional behaviors with-out fear of negative repercussions from their trustees.

For example, funds have sometimes been used for exploratory grants that test the capacity of an inexperienced nonprofit. They have been used to provide emer-gency stabilization support to a nonprofit that was essential to a neighborhood ini-tiative but was crumbling organizationally. Monies have been used as bridge funding for nonprofits awaiting a forthcoming grant. They have been paid as stipends to individuals or as direct-expense payments for informal associations without 501(c)3 status. Funds have been used to support preliminary exploration of promising ideas that were formative or undeveloped, without any guarantee that these ideas would materialize. And they have been used to underwrite resident pressure campaigns that could generate political backlash.

It is worth taking a closer look at one of these risk-taking instances by a funder collaborative. In 1998, LAUF was supporting the creation of a workforce initiative on the platform of school-linked services. A network of school-based parent centers was functioning as "one stops" for a range of family services. The plan developed by local parent groups and other residents was to construct the workforce initiative such that parent centers would function as "intake valves" linking individuals with jobs in the local economy. In order to work, this initiative relied on the participation of a local business assistance agency that possessed extensive, longstanding relationships with manufacturers and retailers throughout the area. No organization remotely possessed the employer relations that this agency had earned over several decades. They were, in the words of more than one funder, "the only game in town."

The problem was that, despite the excellence with which it delivered services, this agency was internally in crisis: Newspaper headlines reported allegations of fiscal mismanagement; the agency had withdrawn from a sizable credit line with no apparent means of repayment; the majority of its board members had submitted their resignations; and within a matter of weeks, its president would depart the organization under contentious circumstances.

No funder would have ever made a grant to an organization in such complete disarray. And yet, on a programmatic level, this organization remained "the only game in town." So LAUF members, agreeing that no one of them would individually make a grant, contemplated whether they were able to take the risk collectively, shoring up a partner of central importance to the neighborhood initiative. They explored ways of protecting their interests: They treated the funding as a month-to-month contract to be managed by LAUF, instead of as a grant; they contracted consultants to provide intensive management assistance aimed at overhauling the financial, personnel, and governance systems; and they placed a LAUF board member on the board of the agency. Within two years, the organization had not only fulfilled all goals in terms of its role in the workforce initiative, but reemerged as one of the most respected and reputable nonprofits in Los Angeles.

Although the greater risks at LAUF were taken by the group, a number of individual funders began making grants related to the neighborhood initiatives that also represented some unconventional decisions. Fledgling or weak organizations began to receive funding because of the essential role they play overall in the initiatives. The California Endowment made a grant to the newly formed Southeast Communities Prevention & Treatment in South Central because it was one of the only organizations expressly addressing the needs of single mothers with drug addictions. Funders began to engage in more proactive grantmaking, creatively engineering or adapting programs to fit with the big picture and seeking out specific nonprofit partners instead of waiting passively for their proposals to come across the transom.

One leap of faith that almost never happens is when foundations go beyond grantmaking to make institutional commitments to a nonprofit effort, complete with nonfinancial contributions. It implies a level of intimacy and commitment that most consider perilous. LAUF members have been called upon to think of themselves not only as grantmakers, but as human links between resource-poor communities and the vast nonfinancial assets that exist throughout our philanthropic and corporate institutions.

Working intimately with nonprofits is itself a risk to many foundations. In such situations, funders run the risk of losing professional distance or creating the incorrect impression that funding will be guaranteed. Such funders risk accusations of favoritism by other organizations. Despite these fears, many collaboratives have attempted to create a more people-centered environment with an emphasis on relationship building, frequent communication, and full disclosure. LAUF members, for example, can now engage easily in funding discussions with nonprofit leaders without thinking of them as "nonprofits at the trough."

For national and statewide foundations, local funder collaboratives reduce risk by blending their funding streams with those of funders who are more familiar with local circumstances. This is true, for example, in Los Angeles, where national foundations have bemoaned the daunting scale and complexity of the region and how impenetrable it can seem to an outsider. LAUF has provided an orienting framework and an instant peer group and support network made up of funders who are well-grounded in the local context. On a national scale, the Funders' Network for Smart Growth and Livable Communities has introduced national funders to nascent funder collaboratives in virtually every metropolitan region of the country.

Another characteristic of funder collaboratives that affects their ability to take risks is the simple fact that they are composed of individuals. Although funder collaboratives are essentially institutional partnerships (a subject to be taken up in greater detail in the next chapter), decisions are nonetheless driven by the individuals assigned to represent their institutions at collaborative meetings. Since collaborative members rarely have explicit instructions or mandates to bring to the table, they must rely on personal judgment, experience, and intuition. As a result, the mix of personalities, the degree of authority that representatives perceive they have been granted by their institutions, and old-fashioned small-group dynamics become prime determinants of the degree of risk taken.

When the representatives at the table are not foundation presidents or trustees, or if they have not been delegated sufficient authority, the collaborative may actually inhibit risk taking. As LAUF underwent a phase where program officers replaced their presidents on the board, Shirley Fredricks, a LAUF co-chair, found this to be the case: "There were suddenly so many more checks and balances when the group attempted to make funding decisions. There were more individuals to express reservations, concerns, or worries."

Jennifer Vannica, president and CEO of the Jacobs Family Foundation and a member of the San Diego Neighborhood Funders, concurs. She has worked in the Market Creek neighborhood of San Diego both through her foundation's independent grantmaking and through the funder collaborative. While she feels that the collaborative has yielded many benefits, it did not facilitate high-risk funding decisions. In fact, all of the truly risky funding decisions she has participated in—such as the predevelopment financing for a problematic twenty-acre land parcel in the neighborhood—were the result of her foundation's entrepreneurial character.

On the other hand, fully empowered individuals can sometimes take risks more readily than institutions. Institutions, by their very nature, tend to be risk-averse because they seek to protect their own inertial longevity. In the policy arena, it is not an accident that ballot initiatives tend to be funded by individual donors as opposed to institutions. Back in the philanthropic world, the example of Social Venture Partners comes to mind. Individual donors, allocating their own personal resources with full information, have demonstrated a remarkable tendency to "roll the dice" with start-up organizations and "wild ideas."

Finally, many funder collaboratives have been able to take risks more easily because their decision making is driven by an individual staff person who is free of bureaucratic limitations and authorized—even encouraged—to act entrepreneurially and creatively. The directors of the Foundation Consortium for California's Children and Youth and LAUF, for example, were explicitly charged with cultivating an environment where members could "think out of the box" and "complicate their thinking."

———————

As a parting thought on the subject of risk, it is worth noting that the vast majority of funders who have participated in risk-taking collaboratives are extremely pleased with the freedom the collaborative structure has provided them. Moreover, many claimed that their grantmaking was directly affected and that they were more comfortable taking risks with their individual grantmaking activities, so long as it was related or adjacent to the activities of the collaborative.

Beyond these coordinated group activities, risk-averse behaviors remained the norm. In other words, although funder collaboratives have become an effective greenhouse for risk and innovation, they rarely alter the risk threshold for philanthropy in their communities. It may be that funder collaboratives are a necessary ingredient in the ongoing mix of philanthropic instruments of every community. They may be a permanent compensatory measure that complements regular grantmaking by continually taking necessary risks and exploring the next generation of innovations, only to hand these innovations off to individual foundations as they become routinized approaches. On Wall Street, investors routinely divide their investment dollars into different categories of risk, creating a mix of diversified investments. Through funder collaboratives, philanthropy can do the same.

CHAPTER 6

Funder Collaboratives as Mechanisms for Better Philanthropic Governance

Philanthropic governance, the process by which funding priorities are established and funding decisions are made, is the subject of this chapter. Most conversations about philanthropic governance relate to the internal workings of individual foundations. Indeed, there is growing pressure on foundations to have more transparent decision-making processes, and there is increased scrutiny related to whether they are adding value and generating returns for their exempt assets.

This chapter will consider the notion of governance *across* foundations, a complicated proposition that is rarely discussed. It will look at philanthropic governance in terms of the way democratic decision making takes place across foundations wherever shared assets or funding coordination is involved. It will consider how such decision making takes place within the funder collaboratives and examine the structures through which such collaboratives engage nonprofits and community constituencies in their decision making.

With so many different approaches to philanthropic governance, cross-foundation governance becomes especially problematic. As with the United Nations, its members place different valence on democracy and have different expectations about how decisions should be made, who should be making them, and how long they should take. Bringing together such diversity in a common decision-making framework requires a neutral platform. There must be no concern about one stakeholder group unduly influencing the policy-making process, or the mutual agreements will dissolve.

Funder collaboratives, then, inevitably raise challenging governance questions. New forms of governance are sometimes necessitated by the fact that funds are removed from individual foundations and then pooled and placed under the oversight of a funder collaborative comprised of representatives of each foundation.

Taking the strategizing and decision-making functions out of the individual foundation boardrooms and putting them into partnerships with other foundations has yielded multiple benefits.

Balance of Power

Aside from the obvious benefits of pooling financial investments and combining knowledge, the funder collaborative creates a constructive balance of power, ideas, and strategies. For this reason, it is still prudent for even a large foundation—such as Ford or Rockefeller—which may have sufficient funds and an adequately multidisciplinary staff, to work in groups for the check-and-balance effect.

When acting alone, a foundation can exert unintentional and undue influence on nonprofits even with the best interests at heart. When nonprofit leaders equate their financial stability with their funder's satisfaction, they are more easily influenced by that funder and may not feel comfortable standing up to the funder's suggestions and recommendations. Desperate for funding, the nonprofit may try to "make it work"—and then face dire consequences. This is why foundations like Ford and Hewlett set term limits on how many years a person can serve as a program officer. No other field would remove a person when they have acquired expertise and depth of experience. But it is seen as a necessary response to the inevitable growth of unhealthy power relations.

In the context of a collaborative, however, when one foundation is advocating a certain direction, the other funders need to "co-sign" or cast "confirming votes" in order for the idea to move forward. Collective strategizing mitigates against the whim of individual foundations. For many collaboratives, a consensus-based model of decision making has entailed negotiating policies and procedures that everyone in the group can comfortably endorse.

For Craig McGarvey, a former member of Los Angeles Urban Funders and Long Beach Funders, funder collaboratives provide a healthy compensatory measure for the "idiosyncratic whims" of individual foundations. "A foundation acting alone can convince itself that what it wants to do is the right thing. But when you are in a room full of peers, there is a built-in self-reflection and criticism. This is what democracy is really all about."

Clearly, some funders would appropriately accrue power within specific debates due to their substantive expertise in the subject at hand. At LAUF, for example, as childcare rose to the fore as an issue in one of the neighborhoods, the foundation with the most knowledge in this area, or the most extensive network of childcare provider grantees, became the most influential person at the table. And when the board faced a series of important funding decisions related to education, those funders with a demonstrated track record in educational grantmaking were given special credence. But the group process would ensure that no one funder would have inordinate influence on the overall decisions.

In funder collaboratives where decisions are made collectively by the funders, each foundation is generally given one vote at the table. This is true, for example, at the Foundation Consortium for California's Children and Youth, the Funders' Collaborative on Youth Organizing, Long Beach Funders, San Diego Neighborhood Funders, Health Funders Partnership of Orange County, and the Trenton Funders Collaborative. The democratic decision-making procedures put in place ensured that all funders have equal power at the table, regardless of the size of their assets or contribution to the fund. Even in a collaborative as large and potentially unwieldy as the one-hundred-plus-member Funders' Collaborative for Strong Latino Communities, each funder has one vote.

LAUF board members concluded that there would be no standard amount donated to the fund, or even a contributions formula. Instead, each funder is asked to contribute to the fund a "grant significant relative to its average grant size." Every foundation, whether large or small, is entitled to two board representatives (one primary, one secondary) and a single vote on all policy issues. Many LAUF members have remarked that LAUF is one of the only settings they know of in which all foundations are equal in status, regardless of the size of their assets. Torie Osborn, the executive director of the Liberty Hill Foundation, explains the benefits that this democratic structure holds for a small foundation like hers: "LAUF has been good for Liberty Hill because we are a little player in terms of the money we can invest, but LAUF made us an equal around the table. This has increased our credibility and support for our work outside of LAUF."

This is not to say that during the early years of LAUF, and again during the years 2000-01 when the pooled fund was being replenished for the second phase, that the group did not recognize how financially essential it was to have the participation of large statewide or national funders. Indeed, special concerted efforts were made to court such funders, which undoubtedly reminded other funders of their financial inequalities. But as the collaborative completed its fundraising and commenced its on-the-ground work, egalitarian values prevailed. And once work in the neighborhoods took form, individual foundations on the board accrued power based on their substantive knowledge base and its relevance to neighborhood problem solving.

Superficially, at least, the Long Beach Funders Collaborative made decisions by democratic consensus among the members of the body. The small size of the group (which ranged from five-seven funders) meant that even when decisions were voted upon, the vote was largely a formality recapping a thorough discussion of the issue among the members. Funds were pooled at an intermediary institution, the Liberty Hill Foundation, which served as a fiscal sponsor and created a symbolic neutral context for decision making. Liberty Hill was not a member of the collaborative.

However, representatives of the two largest foundations were uncomfortable with the level of deference they received from their peers. One of these members explains that "the other funders desperately wanted us at the table, which meant constantly deferring to us. They wanted a regional funder from outside Long Beach, perceiving it to have a legitimizing effect." The other large funder also found the accommodations to her foundation to be uncomfortable. "The other funders acted like grantees around us—not talking to us directly, fearful of losing funding." She suspected (correctly, it seems) that there were meetings going on "about her foundation" outside of regular collaborative meetings.

In short, extra weight was given to larger funders despite the fact that no one, including the larger foundations, seemed to want it that way. These misperceptions might have been mitigated had all promised funds been committed up front, thereby removing any negotiating power based on funding not yet received. Funders frequently wonder whether putting a lot of money on the table corrupts the decision-making process. Undoubtedly, it sometimes does. But in this case, it seems to have been the promise of funds not yet granted that corrupted the decision making. Another helpful strategy would have been for staff to conduct one-on-one interviews with board members and present the aggregate results, without attribution, back to the group before a final decision was made. Although the final discussion would have removed any doubt about where each funder stood, the majority patterns would have been revealed.

Democratic Decision Making

Among existing funder collaboratives, there are numerous alternative structures for group process and decision making. Some are formal foundation consortia that follow stringent procedures for membership, representation, and voting. Others are more flexible and depend on consensus-building techniques to find shared pathways that all funders can agree upon. Others are still looser configurations where each funder retains its own decision-making autonomy but voluntarily coordinates its grantmaking with that of its peers. Increasingly, though, emerging funder collaboratives are hybrids, utilizing different degrees of democratic decision making according to the needs of specific situations. Rather than blindly adopting one model of governance, they are freely combining and recombining approaches, becoming a vibrant, if fragile, laboratory for democratic processes.

The San Diego Neighborhood Funders has utilized formal, democratic voting procedures in managing its pooled fund. But to accommodate the need for individual funders to retain control over some of their grantmaking, the group invented the notion of a "family of funds." This family of funds is a set of categorically restricted funds held at the United Way of San Diego, the same fiscal agent as the pooled fund. In this way, categorical funders can remove funds from their foundation to be allocated, as needed, for aspects of the neighborhood initiatives that fall within their funding guidelines. By preapproving the allocation of these funds, and holding them aside at the United Way, the funders create a system allowing for the co-synchronization of disbursements.

Perhaps the most challenging problem faced by a collaborative is when not all the foundations have made unrestricted contributions to the pooled fund, but have made restricted grants that relate to the work of the collaborative. Denise Dahlhausen, the former executive director of Long Beach Funders, observes that there were funders sitting at the table, making decisions about the pooled fund, who had not contributed to it. Making a restricted grant that is tied to the initiative is not the same as pooling unrestricted funds. Dahlhausen suggests that "foundations should look at their portfolio and decide how much money will be set aside for the big picture—perhaps pooled with others—and how much will go toward direct services. To fully participate in the collaborative, it is critical they make an investment in that big picture."

It is true that many collaboratives, like the Los Angeles Immigrant Funders Collaborative, depended on the upfront staffing and leadership of one foundation (The Emma Lazarus Fund) in order to get started. Beverly Coleman, at the Philadelphia Neighborhood Development Collaborative, explains that one reason so many funder collaboratives in existence today are focused on community development issues is because of the leadership role played by the Ford Foundation: "In the 1990s Ford was instrumental in the development of collaboratives as a model for contributing to the strengthening and sustainability of community development corporations (CDCs). But in the interest of full investment and a collective sense of ownership, it was imperative for all of these collaboratives to develop joint governance."

The functionality of a funder collaborative as a governance structure is based in large part on whether it is a collaborative of individual grantmakers—who happen to represent foundations—or the philanthropic institutions themselves, for whom the individual representative is incidental. This is a critically important distinction because it determines whether the individuals sitting at the table have constituencies they are representing (i.e., their foundation employer) or whether they are individuals who have been preauthorized by their foundations to vote according to their conscience. In the latter scenario, the group can function as an independent decision-making body or it can voluntarily seek out a constituency to whom it will hold itself accountable. In most cases, this would be the grantees or the populations they serve.

Funder collaboratives often learn the importance of having fully authorized, high-level peers sitting around the table. Those funders who had to work through their bureaucracies at home were less able to participate in a timely manner within the collaborative. Serious constraints were forced by individuals who had not been granted complete autonomy and were continually seeking answers to questions being asked internally.

Julie Meenan suspects that "anybody from a foundation limited by bureaucracy probably shouldn't have been at the collaborative. They shouldn't have been at the table discussing the bigger picture, because they would inevitably muddy up the waters." She does not place blame, but empathizes with the frustration. "I think it made some members' experience miserable at times. They would put on their program officer hats and say, 'I want to be clear ... what do I say to my board?'"

Although the role was appropriate, and admirable due diligence for a foundation officer, it limited the ability of the collaborative to act more freely.

Eric Johnson, a member of Long Beach Funders, argues that "if you're going to do a funder collaborative at the program officer level, there's a good chance you won't give the initiative a full chance at success. My view would be to include executive level leadership, or else fully empower the program officers to take risks. Then, if the neighborhood initiative fails, you will at least know that the thing failed on its own merits."

Within the collaborative, staff encountered difficulties maintaining funders at the same level of decision making. One reason was that each board member carried with them a different level of authority granted to them by their represented institutions. "Those with more internal decision-making power were there for the big picture. They were able to focus on larger issues of strategic focus and take greater risks," recalls Julie Meenan.

Another set of tensions arose between the larger, regional foundations and smaller, more local funders. Instead of seeing their differences as complimentary, members admit to reacting critically. Larger foundations began to view the local grantmakers as provincial, due to a perceived lack of information about other national models and comprehensive community-building initiatives. Local funders began to resent the larger ones for drawing superficial conclusions about local, gritty realities.

When it came to disbursing funding, the collaborative members harbored different views depending on whether they were small local funders or large national ones. "The local foundations were looking at the consulting bills and wishing those dollars could be directed toward direct services," explains Denise Dahlhausen, former executive director. "The large funders were more comfortable with these kinds of investments and impatient with local funders' frugality."

In retrospect, it is possible to imagine how these differences might have been capitalized upon in an appropriate division of labor. Eric Johnson sees the rationale for "combining small, engaged, on-the-ground funders with bigger and better-financed institutions." The benefit to the small local funders was that a collaborative could tackle a more ambitious agenda than a local foundation could alone. The benefit to the larger outfits was access to better on-the-ground information and greater efficiency. Careful group facilitation, designed to allow the different types of funders to lead from their strengths, could have underscored the interdependence of the members.

Joint governance can create a stronger sense of philanthropic ownership over initiatives and commitments that are long term. In most cases, an individual foundation board does not feel a sense of ownership or direct responsibility for anything it funds. Boards respond to proposals that come across their transom, and they make funding decisions based on information supplied to them. But they do not claim any particular initiative as part of their own long-term agenda and mission. As a time-limited funder collaborative, however, LAUF only exists because of its joint funding activities. It is a virtual institution, in a way, that only exists in terms of its history of collective decisions. Its members view themselves as fully invested sponsors, not episodic donors. They feel a sense of ownership.

Of course, time-limited collaboratives can present challenges to group ownership, too. At Long Beach Funders, members who came later into the collaborative's lifecycle were not able to fully express their creativity because the scope of the work had been set long before their arrival. What's more, there was a general sense within the group that it was time to demonstrate results. The window of opportunity for experimentation and risk taking had closed. Whatever special circumstances had been created for incubating new ideas and forging new relationships were now disappearing as the traditional pressures of grantmaker accountability and due diligence returned.

Given the endemic reluctance to speak out with different opinions, major decisions are typically not left to open discussion alone in funder collaboratives. The polite culture of philanthropy can leave grantmakers poorly equipped for genuine discourse with one another, especially where there may be conflicting goals. But finding ways to look at the group's various views in the collective allows for a level of detachment that wouldn't have been easily achieved otherwise.

Again, LAUF is a case in point. Early in the process, when board members were more reluctant to voice their opinions, the evaluator played a key role. Utilizing a common interview protocol, she interviewed each member and reported back the overall patterns and trends as well as significant outlier views. Perspectives were reported back to the board in aggregate, without attributing specific views to individuals.

Later, as members became more comfortable communicating with one another, they used processes for ascertaining "degrees of consensus" and forming acceptable compromises. In only a handful of occasions has the board's decision making been based on a vote count—where not all funders agreed with the action taken—and almost all of those were early in LAUF's existence. As a group, their capacity for productive discourse and debate has grown to be quite sophisticated, and a number of board members report that they now bring their collaborative abilities into other venues and funder groups.

Another crucial aspect of the decision-making process has to do with the level of decisions being made. A funder collaborative is basically an extra layer of apparatus overlaid on the regular grantmaking decisions made by individual foundations. The additional transactional and administrative costs only make sense if the collaborative process adds value. The decisions the group is making must be framed in such a way as to make use of the expertise of the collaborative as a group in ways that would not be otherwise utilized. The information they are provided, through written briefing materials, board presentations, and structured site visits, must lay out the issues in a way that helps the group focus on issues that are neither too abstract nor too specific in order to center their attention and maximize their benefit.

Members of one funder collaborative felt that the way information was provided to them throughout the process was uneven, and sometimes incomplete and poorly prepared. But what was more problematic was that this information was not organized with any forethought to the level of decision making that was appropriate for the collaborative to make. Sometimes the discussions hovered around issues of substantive focus where members felt little or no expertise. Alternately, the discussions scrutinized details and timelines, drawing the collaborative into micromanagement.

When decisions were framed at the level of operational detail, it became impossible for the group to utilize its collective knowledge. "We became micromanagers," explains one member, "focusing on details that did not require our entire group's attention." And when the funder collaborative became visibly frustrated with this level of decision making, the responsibilities fell largely on a staff person who did not have the necessary range of skills, or a clearly defined mandate from the collaborative, to assume them.

Funding recommendations are brought before funder collaboratives in a variety of ways. Sometimes a formal proposal is developed by project staff in conjunction with prospective grantees or other groups, or a set of alternatives with advantages and implications clearly laid out. In this case, the staff person's job is to frame the questions and propose solutions at key points. In other cases, grantees and funders participate in joint brainstorming from which funding recommendations emerge. In still other cases, grantee partners approach the collaborative staff with immediate needs or ideas of their own. In contrast to ordinary grantmaking, funder collaboratives are as likely to demonstrate spontaneity and opportunism as deliberate, methodical planning.

Shared Power with Nonfunders

Another aspect of the decision-making process is the extent to which nonprofit perspectives are incorporated into (or excluded from) the decision-making process. If they are to be a credible force for social change, foundations cannot make decisions or set strategies without some accountability to local constituencies, or without strategically constructing strategies on existing work. The inevitable conclusion is that if philanthropic support is to make a difference, its uses need to be determined not on the donor end, but on the constituency end. In managing and administering these funds and making decisions about how the money will be distributed, it is essential to think about who is making the decisions, and what process they are using.

In Long Beach, the nonprofit leaders contend that Long Beach Funders created its own program model and then sought out nonprofits to implement it. Many questioned the logic model from the outset but were not comfortable sharing their concerns early on in the process. They bemoaned the fact that the Long Beach Funders did not seek out the community-based perspectives and competencies in trying to make the best possible decision.

But funder collaboratives can serve as the contexts for even more transformative experiments in philanthropic governance: those that allow funders and nonfunders to make decisions together. Although most funder collaboratives involve only foundation presidents and program officers, a growing number engage key stakeholders who have a legitimate interest in how funds are disbursed, or who have a perspective or knowledge base that is germane to the successful utilization of the funds. Through the Boston Schoolyard Initiative, the mayor of Boston assembled a multilayered funding board that drew on virtually every group with an interest in public schoolyards and playgrounds. This inclusiveness led not only to joint ownership but to a sophisticated division of labor among all of the parties.

The evolution of LAUF's relationship with its communities evolved developmentally over time. During the early site visits, although all LAUF members were committed to working more collaboratively with neighborhoods, there were still implicit and explicit power relationships at work. The relationship grew from mild distrust to a form of open "shuttle diplomacy," managed by LAUF's executive director, to open conversations among stakeholders.

Over time, LAUF moved from seeking input from residents and nonprofit leaders to actually turning over resources with minimal restriction to consolidated groups of community stakeholders. This shift directly corresponded to the increasing maturation of the neighborhood-based collaboratives, and their ability to synthesize and represent the views of multiple community constitutencies. LAUF defined its role, then, as the catalyst that helps neighborhood groups set their own collective objectives, providing them with the resources to do so, and then acts as the custodian of these objectives, holding them accountable for their own outcomes.

As an alternative to mixing funders and their nonprofit partners in one decision-making body, some funder collaboratives are set up as parallel but distinct governance structures to nonprofit collaboratives. This allows for nonprofits to provide collective input into the funders' decision making while preserving funder autonomy. An excellent example is the Funders Forum on Antibiotic Resistance, which emerged organically from an extended series of discussions between interested funders and nonprofits concerned with the deleterious long-term effects of antibiotics on environmental and human systems. Encouraged by the funders, the nonprofits organized themselves into a coalition that develops collaborative nonprofit strategies and helps to divide roles and responsibilities among the collaborative partners.

To organize their support for the nonprofits, the funders organized into a parallel collaborative of their own. Although the collaborative is separately staffed and governed, the two groups work in close cooperation with one another. The Funders Forum not only supports the work of the nonprofit coalition as a whole, but individual member foundations routinely make grants to specific nonprofits to support their particular roles.

In more extreme examples, the funder collaborative delegates full regranting authority to a group of constituents it considers better qualified to make the funding decisions. At the Community Shelter Board in Columbus, Ohio, the funders gave the board the authority and responsibility to make allocation decisions on how to best cater to the needs of the homeless in Columbus. They do not participate in the decision making. This model can also be observed with the San Diego Neighborhood Funders, who gave grantmaking authority over to a group of community leaders. The Funders Forum on Antibiotic Resistance has done the same.

Interactions with Government

One of the most fascinating aspects of philanthropic governance involves the degree to which funder collaboratives interact with government.

Some funder collaboratives define this interaction as an opportunity to create alignment between public and private funding streams. Since many government agencies make grants of one kind or another to nonprofits, it makes good sense for them to sit down together with their philanthropic counterparts to coordinate and blend their investments. Collaboratives provide a safer, collegial environment in which public and private funders can learn from one another and work cooperatively, without the pressure of a head-on partnership between a single foundation and a single government agency.

Public and private funders frequently harbor gross misperceptions about one another, assumptions that evaporate quickly during collaborative discussions. Many private foundations, for example, still see themselves as funders of "pilot projects" that, once proven, can then be incorporated into policy and "brought to scale" by government. This idea remains popular even though it is increasingly less feasible in this age of shrinking budgets. Similarly, government bureaucrats frequently overestimate the magnitude of philanthropic resources and fail to appreciate the more freewheeling and entrepreneurial spirit of many foundations. Collaboratives that put these funders side by side inevitably create better understanding about the interdependence between government and philanthropy as well as how grantmaking that is free of public accountability can institute new kinds of governance that enable it to play highly strategic roles in large social change initiatives. Public funders begin to appreciate that foundations can be more nimble and flexible, and they can operate with long-term views that outlast political administrations.

Partnerships are especially important where human services and community development funding are involved because these are areas where government agencies seem to engage in the most grantmaking. These are also areas where public and private efforts are most likely to overlap. Kim Burnett, the executive director of the Community Development Partnership Network, is in frequent contact with numerous funder collaboratives engaged in community development investments in the low-income communities of Philadelphia, Detroit, New Orleans, and others. According to Burnett, all of its collaboratives involve both private foundations and local government representatives.

Some other funder collaboratives neither seek to assemble foundations and government agencies around the same table nor attempt to blend philanthropic funding streams with those accountable to the public. Instead, they aim to inform or influence the very process of democratic discourse that leads to government priorities in the first place.

Foundations can use numerous strategies to impact public policy. They can fund research, advocacy, organizing, constituency building, and policy networks. Some of these lend themselves more to individual funder action, while others are best undertaken by groups of foundations working collaboratively. Funders who choose to participate in collaboratives often do so because they wish to avoid the impression that they are engaged in direct advocacy or are attempting to influence legislators—a potentially volatile image for many foundation trustees. The funder collaborative provides an insulating intermediating layer, as well as "strength in numbers" and more aggregate resources than any one foundation would likely be able to access alone.

There are several examples of how groups of foundations took collective action in public policy arenas and how the collaborative structure enhanced their effectiveness within those arenas. One excellent example is the Public Policy Institute of California, created by a partnership of the James Irvine Foundation, the Hewlett Foundation, and the Packard Foundation. The Public Policy Institute aims to bring underrepresented perspectives to the forefront of policy debates. They do Spanish-language polling in order to obtain views from an enormous, and often unheard, population in the state. The three funders would not describe themselves as representing a particular political viewpoint; rather, they are simply standing for greater inclusion.

In another California example, the Foundation Consortium for California's Children and Youth works to influence public policy development and implementation on a variety of levels, including state, county, and community. Striving for the increased safety, health, and education of California's children and families, the seventeen foundations that comprise the Foundation Consortium are able to persuade policy decision-makers through the intermediary of the consortium (since foundations are often prohibited from implementing advocacy activities on their own). Therefore, the participating foundation remains behind the scenes, either when struggling for policy change within the government, or growing its grassroots community relationships.

Bonnie Armstrong, of the Foundation Consortium, explains that "collaboratives provide a wonderful opportunity for funders to protect themselves a little in the very risky business of public policy engagement." She adds that, although the Foundation Consortium's funding levels are miniscule relative to government budgets, the Consortium can be highly opportunistic and situational: "We can hire a consultant at a time when government cannot, because of hiring freezes."

The Foundation Consortium has even been able to help the state to leverage federal dollars. The Consortium has contributed resources from its pooled fund to state government, which it can in turn use to draw down some federal matching dollars based on shared goals. Since the state was unable to contribute a single dollar to the effort, the Foundation Consortium support was the decisive factor in its ability to activate the federal support.

Funder Collaboratives as Sources of Innovative Governance

Since no form of governance is perfect, these experimental modes of decision making must be seen not as ends in their own right, but as an evolving process of continuously improving decision making.

Collaborations can demonstrate new modes of decision making for individual foundations. Critics and muckrakers ask hard questions about the composition of boards, how decisions are made, and the right by which board members make funding decisions on behalf of others. Not only are foundation board members not elected by the public, but the mechanisms for their appointment seem mysterious and secretive to the outsider. After all, just because a board has the money doesn't mean it has the authority, capacity, competency, legitimacy, or good judgment to spend it in a way that will achieve the highest philanthropic benefit.

When a foundation is created, the money is placed in a public trust and no longer belongs, in a strict legal sense, to the original donor, family, or corporation. Their direct influence ceases the moment the foundation is incorporated, the funds converted into nontaxable assets, and the mission statement and bylaws finalized. It is then the responsibility of the foundation's board of directors, or other governance structure, to make funding decisions in support of the mission.

Critics also contend that foundation boards have little objective external feedback to help them set funding priorities and future policy directions, and they are too removed from day-to-day work to draw conclusions of their own. One suspects that they rarely reflect the needs of the constituencies being served, but are more likely to represent the interests and values of the original donor. And research has shown that—despite what we would like to believe—most boards offer little or no assistance to the foundation executive and may even serve as barriers to good decision making.

The speed and relative ease with which funder collaboratives can form and re-form could accelerate the learning process, and constituency-based models of decision making could dramatically impact public sector problem solving in the future. It's not far-fetched to imagine that funder collaboratives could one day outpace experiments in governance in the public sector.

Theorists of democratic governance have attributed American voter apathy to the bluntness of majority-rule, winner-take-all politics. Such processes lack nuance and sophistication. They fail to reflect an important reality: that some constituencies are more heavily impacted by certain policy decisions, and therefore deserve additional weight given to their perspectives. Policy issues are often so complicated and overwhelming that voters feel they lack sufficient information to make more than a superficial assessment. But funder collaboratives investing in long-term processes of community engagement, issue identification, and education find they are building a population capable of providing thoughtful input and analytical feedback to philanthropic strategies. Public sector governance could find much worthy of imitation in these efforts.

Any discussion of governance must be predicated on an understanding of the legitimacy of those who govern. What is the basis of legitimacy for the private foundation? Why should large amounts of money be taken out of the tax stream to be spent by a private institution for public purposes of its own choosing? And in funder collaboratives, what good is democratic allocation of resources by multiple funders if none have any legitimacy in their area of pursuit?

Some would counter that there need not be a special argument for a funder's legitimacy. After all, in any civil society, individuals can and should make acts of generosity and charity according to their own free will. But foundations are not individuals. They are privileged institutions that can exist in perpetuity, and are permitted to hold aside assets with tax benefits that imply a value added. The basis of their legitimacy is therefore a valid subject for debate. And as funder collaboratives begin to increase the power, influence, and effectiveness of philanthropy, they increasingly find their place as a subject for this debate.

CHAPTER 7

Funder Collaboratives as Systems for Better Communications and Knowledge Management

There is no denying that we are in the digital age and that the worldwide use of the Internet and cellular technologies has transformed every aspect of society. Whether we are shopping, studying, working, or playing, we now expect information to be communicated to us frequently and succinctly; transactions to be high speed, if not immediate; and services to be responsive to our needs, if not actually customized to them. A philanthropic field that seems mysterious to grantseekers, glacially slow in its decision making, and infrequent—if not utterly negligent—in its public reporting, is anachronistic and out of place.

It has been argued that philanthropy has an obligation to communicate openly about its funding record and the lessons it learns.[1] As a government-regulated industry, philanthropy should be scrutinized by the federal government, as well as state governments, relative to its tax-exempt status. Public disclosure of philanthropic activities is central to a public understanding of foundations' work and the retention of their privileged status. More importantly, there is a moral and ethical obligation for public trusts to be forthcoming with the public.[2] It has also been suggested that more effective communication across foundations with grantees, and with the public at large, can actually serve the self-interest of the individual foundations by helping them to fulfill their mission.

Some foundations have taken up this challenge with enthusiasm: providing their funding guidelines and record of past grantees on websites; making more frequent and accessible reports on their grantmaking; establishing structured feedback mechanisms; and adapting their funding streams to the current needs of nonprofits. Among the more noteworthy is the Schwab Foundation, which has gone so far as to hire a "knowledge management officer" whose responsibilities include researching, writing, and disseminating brief, digestible reports on the foundation's progress.

The application of these strategies is still the exception to the rule, however. Whereas most professional fields are based on a common base of knowledge, philanthropy's decentralized, pluralistic approach to grantmaking undervalues information sharing. In fact, with their different perspectives, philosophies, and capacities, conversations among foundations can be highly unproductive. Grantmakers will frequently end up talking at cross-purposes, contradicting and confounding one another. With so many diverse institutions pursuing their own particular notions of philanthropy, it should not be surprising that they do not talk to each other as much as they should.

Funder collaboratives are of importance to this discussion because they create special opportunities for enhanced communications among foundations and between funders and their grantees. By definition, a funder collaborative depends on intense coordination, communication, and the sharing of knowledge between foundations. It also creates a self-contained laboratory for experiments with new communications systems. A group of funders who have found a point of collaboration become a closed system within which many communications and information management challenges can be worked through. Once again, a funder collaborative can serve as a window into what's possible for the field at large.

Pooling Existing Information

Before launching a new philanthropic initiative, or beginning work in a new realm of grantmaking, it is commonsensical for a funder to gather what is already known by others in the field. For every prospective grantee, there are often dozens of other foundations that have funded them in the past. These foundations will have plentiful information about the grantee's performance, ability to meet objectives, and relative effectiveness of programmatic strategies. Unfortunately, this kind of information gathering is usually sporadic, infrequent, and unsystematic. While the benefits to the grantmaker are obvious, the time involved in identifying informants or interviewing them prohibits any comprehensive fact gathering.

But at a minimum, funder collaboratives can serve as effective vehicles for collecting, archiving, combining, and recombining the data from funders working within specific substantive or geographic areas. At the most basic level, this can be accomplished through structured group conversations where funders "compare notes" with one another. By operating from a common base of knowledge, all members will be better able to coordinate their grantmaking, and they will be aware of the possible pitfalls that may await.

It was for these reasons that the San Diego Neighborhood Funders (SDNF), in selecting a target area for their community initiative, selected the small geographic area surrounding the Market Creek-Euclid Avenue hub. A survey of participating funders revealed that two-thirds of them already had a history of grantmaking within the target area. Several of the funders had even lived or worked in the neighborhood at one time or another. Consequently, the group was able to navigate quite effectively through the local intergroup dynamics and accurately assess the capacities of the local nonprofits.

Another facet of funder communications is the way that established funders share their experience with newer and younger grantmakers. An interesting example can be found at the Jewish Funders Network (JFN), which facilitates working groups serving as both formal and informal means for JFN members to communicate, collaborate, and become more educated about particular areas of interest. One of these is JFN's Younger Funders Collaborative, a learning environment in which next-generation and emerging Jewish philanthropists develop their ability to create impact within their families, foundations, communities, and the world at large, in a way that is informed by Jewish ethics and traditions.

Though the effort is small in scale, its potential impact is significant. The Younger Funders Collaborative, which was initially undertaken as a yearlong shared grantmaking program, awarded $13,800 to Project Enterprise, a business training and microloan organization for low-income New Yorkers. A close group of fifteen members come together to share their passions and gain personal grantmaking experience with a community of peers.

Funder collaboratives also create unique learning opportunities between large national or statewide foundations on the one hand, and the smaller, more local funders on the other. In the case of SDNF, the larger foundation benefited enormously from its access to the better on-the-ground information possessed by the smaller, more local funders. Similarly, through the Local Initiative Funding Partners, the Robert Wood Johnson Foundation can disperse its knowledge around health issues while drawing upon local learnings around implementation in diverse contexts.

There is increasingly a growing number of less formal, less visible funder collaboratives comprised of foundations that happen to be funding the same project or initiative and wish to maximize their learnings from it. These groups tend to call themselves "learning communities" or something similar. There is, for example, the Funders Learning Community made up of foundations supporting the Bay Area School Reform Collaborative.

Shared Research

In addition to information already held by individual funders, there is often original research that needs to be carried out in order to inform the planning for a philanthropic strategy. This might include literature reviews, survey research, environmental scans, focus groups, or other social science methods. Doing these studies properly can be extremely expensive and time-consuming to manage. So if there are multiple funders that will benefit from the research, it is logical for them to undertake the process together. The collective analysis and interpretation of this data leads naturally to its translation into collective practices and policies.

In South Carolina, the Spartanburg County Foundation led a small group of foundations in the development of an initiative now known as "Healthy

Spartanburg." During the earliest stages of collaboration, the funders had difficulty finding common language, a shared knowledge base about local health conditions, and common assumptions about how they could collectively make a difference. Each foundation approached grantseekers with different definitions of health and different performance expectations.

Their first order of business, then, was to carry out a collective learning process in which they shared the cost of gathering data on local health conditions. They held joint meetings of trustees to build inter-foundation rapport and to ensure the full institutional support of the foundations, and they invited experts in public health issues to come to Spartanburg and inform their thinking. This shared learning experience placed all of the funders on relatively even footing, setting the stage for true cooperation later on.

The group then formulated a shared mission statement, a sweeping call to action that defined roles for healthcare providers, policy makers, and community groups. They backed up that mission statement by initiating a countywide dialogue on public health and by making a set of grants to nonprofits that were positioned to help implement the mission statement. None of this ambitious undertaking would have been possible without the existence of a shared base of knowledge.

Other examples abound. The pooling of financial resources makes it possible for the National Funders Collaborative for Violence Prevention (NFCVP) to invest in a level of knowledge collection that no one foundation would likely undertake alone. The NFCVP supports original research into aspects of violence and its prevention, focusing largely on how the media frames violence and how this framing affects public perceptions and policies. This research is critical to the Collaborative's national and local work.

One crucially important finding for the Collaborative's members is that depictions of violence in the media are almost always associated with populations of color, resulting in deep biases that affect how they are treated and how criminal justice policies are framed. Another is that children who are victims of, or witnesses to, violence in their homes frequently show up in juvenile justice systems and again in adult prisons later in life. Additionally, research shows that there is a significant link among all forms of interpersonal violence and that violence in the home—in the form of domestic violence and/or child abuse—contributes significantly to youth and community violence.

These major research efforts have immediate applicability for all of the member foundations and the types of programs and initiatives they fund. Despite the growing evidence that connects violence from early childhood through adulthood, efforts to prevent violence have been segregated by strategy—and few programmatic models exist to address these links. Currently, violence prevention professionals tend to function within the boundaries of their areas of specialization. They rarely address the intersection among all the forms of interpersonal violence or the importance of citizen engagement and community empowerment. Few practitioners and community leaders understand the complexities of all the issues involved. While functioning without communication, cross-training, or partnerships, different organizations and systems frequently serve the same individuals, families, and communities with a fractured approach that seriously impedes real prevention and community building.

As a result, NFCVP launched a national dialogue on ways to forge segregated building strategies. At a meeting convened in February 2000, key experts representing the broad scope of the violence prevention field came together to formulate a plan for building a common agenda linking research on family, youth, and community violence with practice and policy. Central to this process was the opening of communication channels between, and cross-fertilization among, traditionally separate key constituencies. The result had national implications and affected the funding patterns of all the member foundations. But in all likelihood, none of the research on which this common agenda has been built would have fulfilled its real-world potential if it had not been framed as the collaborative project of multiple funders.

Grants Management

Grants management activities, the procedures through which foundations track records of their funding activities, also have much to gain from funder collaboration. Once you begin thinking of a group of funders as a closed system, it becomes feasible to put in place shared grants management systems. With common applications, reporting formats, aligned funding cycles, and integrated databases, it in turn becomes possible to speak of a portfolio of grants that is assembled from disparate funders but that is treated as a coordinated set within a common framework.

One of the best examples is that of the Health Funders Partnership of Orange County. This group of nine foundations and two public funding agencies quickly recognized the importance of systematizing the process by which they made funding decisions. Toward that end, they developed GrantPartners.net, a Web-based clearinghouse for both grantmakers and grantseekers. It works in a straightforward manner. Health-related nonprofit agencies in Orange County submit their 501(c)3 ruling and other backup materials to obtain a log-on ID and password. Once online, they fill out grant applications, which are then available for all participating funders to review. Funders can also log on—anonymously—and sort applications by whatever criteria they choose—zip code, target population, size of request, etc.

Nonmembers of the Health Funders Partnership of Orange County also are invited to use GrantPartners.net. In fact, the site is particularly appealing to individual donors who have no staff to administer grant applications. The system is currently focused on the interests and geographies of the Health Funders Partnership, but can easily be enlarged to encompass more foundations over time. It is easy to imagine that, over time, a universal Web-based system could be established for the philanthropic and nonprofit sectors. But it is hard to imagine the process ever getting started without groups of funders trying it out first on a smaller scale.

The Community Shelter Board (CSB) offers an excellent example of how philanthropic collaboration can result in more effective knowledge management and information systems at the service delivery level. The CSB has created an extensive database on both homeless service providers and their clients (who often migrate from provider to provider). This information has allowed CSB to better understand the city's homeless services system as a whole and better understand how their funding can be most strategically deployed to benefit the entire system. Over the years, CSB has developed a unique intermediary role between funders and grantees, smoothing the fundraising and funds management activities for agencies while improving accountability to funders.

At a national level, the National Education and Research Forum (NERF) Funders Forum was set up in 2001 in the United Kingdom. The Funders Forum was established to address an underlying lack of communication among funders of educational research that resulted in a lack of balance between short-term and long-term priorities, and between the diverse interests of policy makers, practitioners, and researchers.

The Funders Forum set out to accumulate the most recent educational research from universities, institutes, research centers, and foundations, and then to centralize this research for immediate access and application. They have invested in the consolidation of this data and its organization around the following practical themes: quality, impact, funding, priorities, capacity building, evidence base, and key players. This information can be accessed on the Funders Forum website, which also includes links to every funder's individual research products.

Public Campaigns

Collaboratives can, and have, used communications strategies to do more than rationalize information flow among funders or between funders and nonprofits. They have also demonstrated a readiness to take on highly visible, program-related communications campaigns. Everyone is now familiar with the well-known public service announcements on topics such as drunk driving, cigarette smoking, teen pregnancy, pollution, HIV/AIDS, domestic abuse, and nutrition. These types of campaigns are large and costly, and more and more foundations are choosing to take them on collaboratively.

For example, to raise awareness of children's needs for their fathers, the Annie E. Casey Foundation, Danforth Foundation, Kansas City Community Foundation, and Mott Foundation worked over a two-year period with Steege/Thomson Communications public relations firm. They organized a White House event and a panel discussion at the National Press Club in Washington, D.C. These campaigns led to stories on the front page of the *New York Times* and in *USA Today*, a thirty-minute interview on CNN, a segment on *The NewsHour with Jim Lehrer*, and in scores of other outlets nationwide. The example of NFCVP is again relevant. In the wake of the recurring violence in communities across the country, the NFCVP and other national violence prevention organizations need to be able to develop messages of violence prevention and to communicate them to a broad public.

Research has indicated that journalists and their audiences—not to mention policy makers and their constituents—need to be educated about the biases in the media related to crime and violence. These findings have implications for the development of both proactive and communications strategies (that help address biases before incidents occur) and reactive strategies (that enable journalists to respond in a clear-headed way when stories break).

Another communication strategy that can only be undertaken collaboratively is the communication of philanthropy's role in society to the media and other external audiences. Philanthropy is grossly absent from most news coverage, despite its significant contributions to myriad social concerns. When it is discussed publicly, philanthropy's role is, at best, trivialized; and at worst, misrepresented. Learning to explain philanthropy to a society that is largely unaware of it will take a great many collaborative communications strategies.

Scope and Scale

The scope of knowledge being managed by a funder collaborative can create information overload for its members, especially given the limited size of most collaboratives. But at the same time, the shared information systems being established within many funder collaboratives are among the most "scaleable" aspects of their work. As systems modeled by smaller groups of funders are enlarged and made permanent by existing philanthropic infrastructure organizations, they can achieve significant and widespread impact.

Another way of bringing information sharing "to scale" involves universities, institutes, and research centers. From 1993 through 1996, the AIDS Task Force (now the AIDS Partnership California) pooled knowledge among funders, nonprofits, and universities to create a new model for HIV intervention projects. The collaboration involved researchers at the University of California, San Francisco, who served as evaluators, and nonprofit agencies that operated the projects. This three-way collaboration provided learning opportunities for each partner (e.g., the community agencies learned evaluation methods that they could also use when applying for other project funding), as well as a viable model for providing AIDS education services to various at-risk populations. After a Ford Foundation evaluation of the original eleven programs in this partnership, a lessons-learned document was published. The collaboration was replicated in Chicago and New York.

Partnering with academia can yield much more than information interpretation and analysis—it can facilitate new theories for action and even new fields of endeavor. The Aspen Institute Roundtable on Community Change is a vivid example of funders coming together with academics and researchers to not only reflect on shared learnings, but to mold these learnings into the creation of a whole new field of nonprofit endeavor. The member foundations have sustained a lengthy, in-depth discussion resulting in the publication of numerous monographs and books.

Through collaborative writing and research methodologies, funders and nonprofit leaders are directly engaged in the preparation of these products for dissemination. The usefulness of collaborative information systems is dependent on the quality of the information. To put it crassly: garbage in, garbage out. Foundations are not as rigorous as they could be in collecting data that might be useful to others. When reading a foundation's annual report, it is sometimes difficult to discern its purpose or intended audience. Annual reports have a kind of storytelling quality at best; sometimes, their authors would have you believe that the outcome of the foundation's work was to give away grants. But in a profession where these information systems are fully activated, standards would need to be raised.

The illustrative funder collaboratives explored in this book provide a glimpse into the vast intellectual resources that can be released through funder collaboration. There is every reason to believe that the twenty-first century can witness widespread consolidations of foundation-held information and that a new generation of philanthropic leadership will tackle the monumental challenges of cataloguing, synthesizing, and interpreting this information and designing the systems through which it can be accessed and applied in the real world. Taken as a whole, this information base could measure up to that of modern research universities. Though less rigorous from a social science perspective, the experiential knowledge amassed by funders and their nonprofit partners (once scrubbed clean of the self-congratulatory tone permeating many foundation reports) has the virtue of being drawn directly from practice.

In fact, by collaboratively gathering its own intellectual resources, philanthropy can pursue a whole new set of working relationships with academia, relationships that exploit the benefits of each field and bridge theory and practice in new ways.

Notes

1. The ideas in this chapter were developed during the "Marco Polo" inquiry that was convened by Marcia Sharp in San Francisco between 1998-2001. This extended discussion among foundation leaders focused on the role of communications, information systems, and knowledge management in philanthropy.
2. Parachini, Allan. "Communication Key to Foundations' Prosperity." *The Chronicle of Philanthropy* 12, no. 23 (September 21, 2000): 55-56.

CHAPTER 8

Funder Collaboratives as Direction Setters for the Foundation World

More than any other sector, philanthropy is equipped to respond to new issues and challenges as they emerge in human society. As explained in chapter 1, foundations are largely free from external accountabilities and can, at least theoretically, respond nimbly and flexibly to any problem as it arises.

But grounded as they are in traditions, trusts, and endowments, foundations frequently circumscribe their own mission statements from the outset. Many American foundations are guided by missions authored a century ago, at a time when many present-day problems could never have been foreseen. And the absence of external accountabilities means that there is little pressure on foundations to regularly reassess their priorities.

From time to time, an individual foundation that has identified a pressing new issue will attempt to bring the issue to the attention of its peers in the hope of per-suading them to rally around the cause. These efforts have limited success. Few foundations are prepared to subvert their own interests and agendas to those of another, solitary funder.

But a *group* of funders is something else entirely. When a collection of funders begins to coalesce around a new issue, foundation executives and trustees are less inclined to dismiss that issue as the particular concern of a single funder. The convergence of interests represented by a collaborative impels them to ask hard questions about the relevance of their grantmaking to an ever-changing world. Funder collaboratives, then, can function as vanguardists—direction setters for the philanthropic field. Like a bird that alters direction, only to have the entire flock follow suit, a funder collaborative can shift resource flows toward new priorities.

Why is this true? Part of the answer lies in a collaborative's freedom from insti-tutional restriction, its predilection for risk, and the creative mix of grantmaker perspectives that have been described in earlier chapters. And part of the reason lies in a funder collaborative's collective prestige, the amalgamation of the reputations of all its member foundations, a force that can represent considerable influence on others in the field. Funder collaboratives can even exert a certain measure of peer pressure. Taken to their logical conclusion, collaboratives can literally transform the philanthropic landscape and its funding patterns, compensating liberally for the inertial tendencies of individual funders. This combination of a collective will to follow uncharted courses, and the potential influence on peers, is what enables these collaboratives to set new directions for philanthropy.

Creating Resources for New Strategic Approaches

There are a number of new, emerging, or resurfacing societal issues around which this dynamic can be observed. Take, for example, the recent flood of research around youth programs and the striking evidence that programs *serving* youth may be less effective than those that develop leadership abilities *within* youth. This is a revolutionary insight in a field that routinely funds youth counseling, drug interventions for teenagers, after-school tutoring, sex education classes, and highly structured extracurricular activities. The implication is that rather than supporting predesigned programs, funders should invest in young leaders who can organize their peers around efforts of meaning to them.

Driven by these ideas, the Funders' Collaborative on Youth Organizing (FCYO) was conceived as a deliberate and strategic attempt to increase available funding for young activists and organizers. For the founding members (the Ford Foundation, Edward W. Hagen Foundation, Jewish Fund for Justice, Merck Family Fund, Open Society Institute, Rockefeller Brothers Fund, and Surdna Foundation), youth organizing represented an important and innovative approach to cultivating young leaders while addressing pressing social issues.

The FCYO conducted an analysis of all funding silos that related in some way to youth organizing or youth development, as well as funding patterns in seemingly unrelated disciplines that might indirectly relate to the work of youth organizers. "Based on what we learned," explains Robert Sherman, a founding member from the Surdna Foundation, "the funder collaborative looked at how to convert funders into youth organizing funders. We had a target market, and we tried to persuade them to shift some of their resources and change how they are spent, thereby breaking down some silos. This is something that an individual funder can probably not do. But a group of funders with the heft to publish, attend conferences, etc., can do it."

In the 1950s, when federal mortgage subsidies and construction of this country's highway network were instituted to foster the development of residential suburbs, few gave thought to the long-term implications of unchecked growth. A half century later, the effects of sprawl are apparent: expansion into environmentally fragile lands; overdependence on the automobile and oil; fiscal burdens on municipalities trying to keep up with infrastructure needs; and deepening divides along racial and class lines.

The Funders' Network for Smart Growth and Livable Communities is a network of foundations that has coalesced around the need to advance social equity, improve neighborhood economies, create livable communities, and protect and preserve natural resources. In partnership with communities, the funders are educated on the causes of inequitable development patterns and how policy makers can respond. The Network then invests in initiatives and policy agendas that promise to strike a more equitable balance across communities within a region. In doing so, they are helping to invent the new field of "smart growth" land development.

The Funders' Network strives to be a focal point for foundations, nonprofit organizations, and other partners to cooperate in addressing the environmental, social, and economic problems created by suburban sprawl and urban disinvestment. It keeps funders informed of critical policy and grassroots developments; enables program staff to share effective strategies and tools; builds the capacity of key constituencies to promote smart growth principles; and raises awareness about the interdisciplinary nature of these issues and the need for sustained engagement by a diverse coalition of funders.

For example, since 1996, the Network has supported a multiphase project lead by the Council of Michigan Foundations to more fully develop and utilize resources available though local community foundations for environmental grantmaking in the Great Lakes. As late as the mid 1990s, when environmental degradation had reached alarming levels in the region, community foundations have been an underutilized resource for environmental grantmaking in the region.

The Great Lakes Community Foundation Environmental Collaborative (GLCFEC) now includes more than thirty-eight community foundations in the Great Lakes region who are learning how to make environmental grants that find local solutions to regional problems. The group seeks to develop a portfolio of grants that may lead to innovative regional strategies that restore ecosystem integrity and prevent losses where the ecosystem's health is threatened. These cutting-edge projects do not fit the current interest categories of the member foundations, but have the potential to provide leadership by exploring out-of-the-box solutions to problems or issues that are only now just being recognized as threats to the health of the Great Lakes ecosystem.

These grants also explore management actions that target newly recognized "master variables"—where minor changes significantly affect ecosystem integrity; or, they may approach an existing issue or problem from a completely new perspective, with the potential for paradigm shifts that result in significant improvements to the health of the Great Lakes ecosystem.

Creating Resources for Underserved Minorities

Aside from focusing on new issues and state-of-the-art strategies, funder collaboratives have created funding streams to serve a number of underrepresented minorities. Among the strong examples are the Funders' Collaborative for Strong Latino Communities and the Los Angeles Immigrant Funders Collaborative. In each case, a relatively small nucleus of funders has sent ripple effects through philanthropy, redirecting funds toward minority groups.

The Funders' Collaborative for Strong Latino Communities was created to strengthen the infrastructure of the Latino nonprofit sector and to cultivate the next generation of Latino leadership. Its conviction is that the explosive growth in the Latino population has not been met with a commensurate increase in nonprofits serving Latinos, and individual foundations operating on their own have not acted upon this unmet need. The Collaborative has therefore set out to create funding streams for this purpose and to educate its members, as well as other funders, on the issues facing Latino communities.

The Collaborative calls itself "the first ethnic-specific funder collaborative" in the country. Started in 2000, the Collaborative set out to raise $16.5 million over five years to strengthen the infrastructure of the nonprofit sector and to cultivate the next generation of Latino community leaders. Despite some initial skepticism that the funds could be raised within that timeline, the Collaborative amassed $17.3 million in just three years, and grew its staff from a single person to three national directors and seven regional coordinators.

A core group of national funders contributed to a pooled fund, which was allocated to regional funder collaboratives on a one-to-one matching grant basis. If a group of foundations in Chicago, for example, were to collect $500,000, the national fund would match that with another $500,000. The intent was to motivate foundations in regions with sizable Hispanic populations to mobilize resources and direct them to Latino-led nonprofits. More specifically, funds were disbursed as a combination of core operating grants for these nonprofits and direct technical assistance to strengthen their performance.

A national board, or assembly, sets the governance and grantmaking policy of the Collaborative. Funds are disbursed at the regional level by local site committees comprised of local and national funders, and a representative from the HIP board of directors. One way the Collaborative influences philanthropic giving is by creating small peer groups of funders in regions where there are substantial Latino populations, but little or no dedicated funding for nonprofits serving them. A site is a geographic area where there are at least two local funders and where at least $250,000 has been raised for grantmaking.

Through this approach, the Collaborative has sparked significant grantmaking in Illinois, California, Colorado, Connecticut, Massachusetts, Rhode Island, New Mexico, New York, North Carolina, Pennsylvania, Wisconsin, and Florida. It is difficult to imagine a single foundation, even with the most charismatic president, achieving such a feat in a few years. Within the first eighteen months of its existence, the Collaborative had attracted nearly one hundred foundations and donors.

The long-term goal of this collaborative is to sustain and ensure the viability of the Latino nonprofit sector and to develop a new cadre of Latino leaders and nonprofits with the vision and capacity to serve their communities. Funds are not used to make routine grants for programs, an activity that any one foundation could readily take on alone. Instead, funds are used to provide hands-on technical assistance, leadership training, and networking opportunities to the leaders of Latino organizations. In this way, the organizations can gain greater visibility within the philanthropic field and attract the attention and support of funders that are not part of the Collaborative. They can eventually achieve the stature and performance of older, more established organizations.

In regions like Los Angeles, where multi-generational Latino communities are well-established and Latinos occupy leadership positions within major foundations, the challenge for the Funders' Collaborative is more manageable. Local foundations already funded Latino nonprofits as a matter of course. They were attracted more by the leverage effect of the matching grant policy than by the chance to seriously alter or redirect their grantmaking. But in other regions, where Latino immigration is a more recent phenomenon, the enormous role of the Funders' Collaborative has been dramatic.

For example, in the four years prior to the formation of the Funders' Collaborative, North Carolina had experienced a 400 percent increase in its number of Latinos, primarily monolingual recent immigrants. However, not a single North Carolina foundation had a Latino program officer. Regional foundations were grateful for the chance to share the resources and expertise of national foundations that were experienced in funding Latino immigrant communities.

Today, there are a number of Latinos in key foundation positions, and the level of funding for the Spanish-speaking communities of North Carolina has been significantly elevated. Moreover, as a result of the peer network inherent in this work, North Carolina foundations resolved to form their own statewide association of grantmakers.

The Los Angeles Immigrant Funders Collaborative is committed to providing assistance to Los Angeles County nonprofits that are focused on the well-being of immigrant and refugee communities. Needs such as healthcare, education, and economic development are often addressed in "gateway" neighborhoods where immigrants first arrive. The Immigrant Funders Collaborative also seeks to support nonprofits tackling policy issues affecting the lives of immigrants. Finally, the Collaborative tries to recruit foundations that contribute to overall community improvement, but whose grants have not necessarily reflected a focus on immigrant and refugee needs.

Significantly, the Funders Collaborative was catalyzed by initial support from the Emma Lazarus Fund. Observing Los Angeles from a distance, the initial funder was convinced that regional funders had not adequately responded to the challenges posed by immigration. But rather than launching its own social marketing strategy aimed at funders, the Emma Lazarus Fund wisely assumed a less central position. It made a seed contribution to a pooled fund, challenging other funders to join. In this way, the identity of the fund was not strongly tied to the Emma Lazarus Fund; ownership was shared among all the funders.

The Collaborative influenced the giving of some large foundations by making it possible for them to fund smaller organizations than they could have supported otherwise. Many of the nonprofit organizations that are most firmly embedded in immigrant communities are small, grassroots start-ups with little or no track record and minimal infrastructure. For the California Wellness Foundation, for example, such organizations would be well below the radar screen. By forging relationships with these groups, the foundation's vision and network of potential grantees has been expanded.

The Collaborative also engages grantees in a highly interactive process designed to identify the ways that foundations can most effectively fund them. In particular, nonprofits have engaged in a push-and-pull exchange around the most effective forms of nonprofit technical assistance. Similarly, the Funders' Network for Smart Growth actually creates a movement by joining forces with a wide range of civic groups and community constituencies. By allowing the lines between funder and nonprofit to blur, philanthropic leaders become more open and receptive to change.

On occasion, there have been organized attempts by nonprofits and community-based organizations to influence the grantmaking priorities and directions of foundations. There are a handful of examples related to community-based organizations—mostly who felt they had nothing to lose—that stridently applied pressure to foundations in an effort to create or redirect funding streams. However, so long as nonprofits are dependent on foundations for their existence, such defiance is likely to remain rare.

But under the right circumstances, as with the Los Angeles Immigrant Funders Collaborative, groups of funders can invite and receive genuine criticism from nonprofits, without creating the same dynamic. They can do this by framing a dialogue with grantees that is generalizable to the state of philanthropy, as opposed to the performance of a particular funder. In this context, grantee censure can be taken as a general commentary on the philanthropic field, and not an attack on a particular foundation or its staff. The funder collaborative can then process the feedback and communicate it in a palatable way to foundation peers.

Moving Resources into Underserved Geographies

The National Rural Funders Collaborative (NRFC) seeks to expand the funding base for impoverished rural communities. Founded in 2001, its goal is to leverage $100 million in public and private funding. It was an outgrowth of the Neighborhood Funders Group (NFG), an affinity group of foundations focused on urban neighborhoods of concentrated poverty. A number of NFG members came together around the recognition that rural communities faced poverty levels as serious as those in cities, but were seriously underfunded.

The NRFC resolved to create new funding streams in rural areas by using its pooled funds to support funder collaboratives in every rural region of the United States. NRFC issued a request for proposals that required multiple partners to come together around a common strategy and agreed-upon outcomes. These local collaboratives needed to include a mix of funders, both private and public, as well as non-profit practitioners and community leaders. The logic was that it was insufficient to simply attract one-time matching funds; there needed to be collaborative structures for mobilizing, coordinating, and directing funds on an ongoing basis.

In selecting its funding recipients each year, every effort was made to assemble a "portfolio" of rural collaboratives that represented a mix of diverse geographic regions, partnership structures, and strategies for alleviating rural poverty. In the first round of funding, twenty regional collaboratives were selected.

Taken collectively, this portfolio of investments comprises what NRFC members refer to as a "learning network" and a "laboratory" for distilling lessons and formulating best practices drawn from real experience. Through an annual assembly, semi-annual convenings of regional and national funders, working groups, and periodic publications or presentations, NRFC synthesizes the experiences of the initiatives it funds. These lessons and best practices are translated into the basis for policy recommendations and new philanthropic guidelines.

In a relatively short time span, NRFC has funded a multitude of collaborative initiatives in every part of the country. These initiatives have leveraged funds within each of these regions and cultivated local philanthropic leadership committed to the new strategies.

These cases suggest that philanthropic innovations that emerge from a web of diverse organizations instead of just one may have greater success at achieving scales of impact. This is because there is more likely to be an emergence of multiple leaders, as well as multiple centers of impetus and broader support than just a single philanthropic clique. Also, the group is more likely to use broader and more all-embracing language for wider appeal. By being essentially network-based, each of these collaboratives has taken a new idea and, through the diversity of its membership, adapted that idea into a multitude of forms.

CHAPTER 9

Conclusion:
Toward a Self-Organizing Philanthropic Field

In these first few years of the twenty-first century, the reasons that have impelled foundations to collaborate have become more prevalent, not less. The explosion in the number of foundations has produced what Lucy Bernholz terms "regions of philanthropic intensity and unprecedented concentrations of funding entities."[1] These entities are likely to be smaller, effectively fragmenting, and disintegrating philanthropic resources.

Further, there is an ever-increasing disparity between the increasingly comprehensive, multidisciplinary understanding of societal problems and the specialized, categorical character of funding streams. Far from making circumstances easier for the nonprofit sector, a crowded funding community is generating even more confusion and conflict of purpose.

And now more than ever, there is evidence that funder collaboration yields demonstrable benefits. Specifically, the previous six chapters have shown how real-world funder collaboratives are producing

- greater efficiencies through shared overhead and planning, as well as reductions in duplication of effort;

- comprehensive arrays of funding streams and categorical specializations, making possible more holistic responses to societal problems;

- the conditions for responsible risk taking by spreading the potential costs of high-risk/high-yield endeavors;

- new forms of decision making that promote cross-foundation dialogue and engage a wider range of stakeholders;

- consolidated information management systems, creating shared fields of knowledge across foundations; and

- peer-to-peer dynamics that can direct funds toward emerging social issues lying outside existing funding categories.

Given the increased relevance of funder collaboratives and the compelling demonstrations of their efficacy, philanthropy has a fundamental obligation to pursue such collaboratives on a wider scale. The goal is not to monolithically promote collaboration for its own sake. If philanthropy is to continue to benefit from its unique ability to differentiate and innovate, then it would make little sense for funders to homogenize in that way.

A more sensible goal would be to create a supportive system where funders are more likely to self-organize freely. The desired state would be one where funders organize themselves into groupings and networks that share information and take collective action on a situational basis. It would be an environment where individual foundations find specialized roles in relation to one another. And it would be one where constituencies and alliances could form and re-form, where efforts could merge and disband according to needs outside the closed system, in the real world. To accomplish this, there would need to be an infrastructure equipped to continually scan the environment for opportunities for private foundations to coalesce around an issue, inject its funding in a coordinated and time-sensitive manner, and make a difference.

Individual Funders That Promote Collaboratives

Sometimes, an individual funder can stimulate the creation of funder collaboration around specific issue areas. The Robert Wood Johnson Foundation (RWJF), for example, seeds funding collaboratives aimed at promoting community-based projects that improve health and healthcare for underserved and at-risk populations. These projects typically represent a fresh approach to improving health and healthcare, one that has not been previously attempted in that community. These community-based efforts may involve forming coalitions, creating new programs, significantly expanding a promising endeavor, or otherwise engaging in new behaviors.

Through its funding partnership with the Local Initiative Funding Partners (LIFP), the Robert Wood Johnson Foundation provides grants of $100,000 to $500,000 per project, which must be matched dollar for dollar by groups of local grantmakers in various regions around the country. The matching funds are awarded through a competitive process that begins when a project is nominated by a local funder according to the guidelines specified by Robert Wood Johnson. Since 1988, RWJF has established partnerships with more than 1,000 local grantmakers to fund 220 projects across the United States. Matching dollars with local funding coalitions, the Foundation has awarded $71 million in LIFP grants.

Driven by the Robert Wood Johnson Foundation, these collaboratives are not as egalitarian as other models. But the relationship definitely strikes a balance between RWJF promoting its interests and the local funding coalitions leading the development of the specific strategies to be funded. The Foundation is particularly interested in programs that address childhood obesity, racial and ethnic disparities in health and healthcare, and services for vulnerable populations, and it advocates for these issues to receive attention. Specifically, proposals must fall within one of the four priority areas: ensuring that all Americans have access to quality healthcare at reasonable cost; improving the quality of care and support for people with chronic health conditions; promoting healthy communities and lifestyles; and reducing the personal, social, and economic harm caused by substance abuse—tobacco, alcohol, and illicit drugs.

But the activities funded invariably reflect the priorities of local funders in concert with RWJF's interest in health and healthcare. The Foundation invites grantmakers to recommend promising projects for this funding partnership. The first step for a nonprofit organization seeking funding under this partnership is to discuss its proposal with a local funder that then may choose to nominate the project. Initiatives that receive a strong endorsement from a local grantmaker are especially encouraged to seek funding.

Infrastructure for the Cultivation of Collaboratives

There are a number of possible institutions with a vested interest in the performance of foundations that could potentially play a role in this system. For instance, a growing number of universities and academic research institutions have assumed responsibility for tracking philanthropic data and convening foundation leaders around pressing issues that surface. Governments at the metropolitan/city level increasingly seek to attract the interest of private and corporate foundations as co-funders of public initiatives. Within specific regions, certain foundations are attempting to become neutral philanthropic players or leaders among their peers. Community foundations, in particular, have demonstrated their interest in serving as vehicles for organizing and directing philanthropic resources.

But there are more obvious choices. As the first chapter describes, philanthropy possesses an extensive, if underutilized, infrastructure that includes national networks and affinity groups and regional associations. It makes good sense to view these existing institutions, especially regional associations, as the most promising place to start. They are a natural asset to build on in that they represent an in-place network of funders that are already familiar with one another and accustomed to interacting with one another. Below are suggested roles to be played by some of these infrastructure institutions.

Regional Associations

Unfortunately, the stance of regional associations has traditionally been oriented toward membership services that offer activities such as professional development training, networking events, and educational seminars and workshops. They have resisted playing a proactive leadership role in helping to catalyze the self-organization of groups of funders to take collective action on particular issues, coordinate their investments in specific geographies, or take advantage of opportunistic circumstances. Nationwide, members openly question whether their associations should be in the business of starting funder collaboratives. They argue that regional associations should be concerned with providing responsive member services, such as workshops and conferences, around issues identified by members. The extra level of staffing support required to convene funders and help them to take collective action feels uncomfortably proactive to some.

As mentioned earlier, this situation is not unique to philanthropy. In any field, membership associations shy away from any leadership stance that could displease a large subgroup of its constituency base. Regional associations of grantmakers are no exception. And yet, such groups often adopt mission statements aimed at "improving the effectiveness of private grantmakers," "creating networking opportunities," and sometimes even "fostering funder collaboration." The challenge seems to be not the ideal of funder collaboration, but the practical realities of having one group of funders appear to be more important, or at least more heavily serviced, than other association members.

However, if the benefits of collaboratives outweigh the obstacles, there are ways to frame and construct funder collaboratives workably within most associations. Successful associations have learned to make an obvious but important distinction: that the association supports any group of members to come together around any issue area as the needs arise, and for whatever duration they deem necessary. It is not the particular funding priority that the association is supporting, but the practice of collaboration itself. In this light, an association could actually be supporting two collaboratives that are advancing agendas on opposite ends of the political spectrum. The association remains neutrally committed to the effectiveness of all of its members.

Another tactic for avoiding the appearance of favoritism is for the association to set as policy that it will recover all costs it incurs as the fiscal sponsor or institutional base of the funder collaborative. Each group of funders wishing to work collaboratively will negotiate a reimbursement fee. An entrepreneurial association may actually generate revenue to be used as a seed fund for formative collaboratives, or for some other discretionary purpose.

If committed to the notion of strategic funder collaboration, regional associations could provide a range of strategies, framed as "member services" if necessary, that could create a pool for the continuous incubation of funder collaboratives, continually fed by streams of fresh information. Most of these strategies are logical extensions of the kinds of services regional associations currently provide; for example,

- Association staff can convene large-scale annual or semiannual conferences where specialists and experts from multiple disciplines analyze socioeconomic trends characterizing the current landscape. The purpose is not merely to analyze problems, but to identify the strategic windows of opportunity where an injection of pooled or coordinated funds could achieve significant impact.

- Staff can meet with groups of funders around these opportunities and offer support to help them develop workplans and to choose an appropriate form of collaboration. Since association staff typically have an in-depth and circumspect familiarity with member interests, they are ideally positioned to proactively handpick groups of funders that may find synergies around common interests.

- Association staff can institute a fund accounting system that allows for the easy fiscal administration of a multitude of funds, with appropriate fees charged for varying degrees of management.

- Staff can maintain interactive databases tracing the relative flow of philanthropic resources into specific issue areas or geographies. This information can help direct responsive and collaborative migrations of funding to where it is needed.

- As an umbrella entity, the regional association can cross-fertilize learnings from one funder collaborative to another, both in terms of the substantive knowledge gained and the insights into the collaborative process.

To provide these services, the regional association would require a new brand of leadership. Executives would need to strike a new balance between supportive servant-style leadership and proactive direction-setting styles. The core group of individuals trained in event coordination and program development, who serve as the full complement of staffing in most regional associations today, would need to be extended to engage a wide range of consultants and specialists who could act as resource persons for collaboratives. The nucleus staff would also need to be trained and skilled in facilitation, group management, and conflict resolution.

Instead of operating like a small or medium-sized nonprofit, as virtually all regional associations do, these innovative associations would need to become larger financial management intermediaries, capable of pooling, aggregating, segregating, tracking, managing, auditing, and reporting on a multitude of funds that arise and disappear as needed. They must be equipped to serve as the mechanism for reorganizing and rechanneling philanthropic dollars on a scale and level of complexity heretofore unseen.

National Funder Affinity Groups and Networks

National networks and affinity groups are at once more challenging and more promising than regional associations. The geographic spread of their membership inherently limits frequency of interaction, but the magnitude of resources they represent can be mind-boggling. And their national scope positions them as the philanthropic counterparts to national networks in other sectors.

Suppose, for instance, that a particular strategy necessitated that philanthropic influence be used to mobilize national social movements within the membership of constituency groups like the American Association of Retired Persons (AARP); the National Association of People with AIDS; the National Association of Social Workers (NASW); the National Association for the Advancement of Colored Persons (NAACP); the National Association for the Advancement of Hispanic Persons (NAAHP); the National Association of People with Disabilities (NAPWD); the National Association of Independent Artists; the National Association of Working Women; or the National Association of Minorities in the Media, to name a few. Only national-level funder collaboratives could forge a true partnership with associations like these.

Or suppose that there was to be a philanthropic influence on the environmental policies of groups like the National Association of Chemical Distributors; the National Association of Petroleum Manufacturers; the National Association of Environmental Districts; the National Association of Ink Manufacturers; the National Association of Electrical Manufacturers; the National Association of Toxic Remediation; or the National Petrochemical and Refiners Association. Only an analogous association of environmental funders could effectively sit down at the table with such groups to propose co-investments in new products, services, or research agendas.

And consider the possibilities of philanthropic partnerships between the U.S Department of Housing and Urban Development around matters of neighborhood revitalization; the Bureau of Indian Affairs around the conditions of Native American reservations; or the Department of Education around school-linked services. Joint ventures undertaken with groups of interested funders could have unprecedented large-scale influence.

Many national funder affinity groups have already helped teams of their members contemplate and pursue such dialogues. But for these affinity groups to cultivate action-oriented collaboratives that are national players, internal changes need to take place within them:

- Annual meetings of the affinity groups must be organized around national scans of the most recent national movements and activities within their field of interest.

- These annual discussions must also include inventories of the key players and an analysis of the "windows of opportunity" wherein a strategic investment of capital or the perceived influence of a national network of funders could have an impact.

- The directors and executive committee members of these affinity groups must dedicate both the time and resources to networking among their counterparts in other sectors, attending annual meetings of other networks as official delegates of the affinity groups. They must cultivate skills in high-level negotiation, diplomacy, and statesmanship.

- These affinity groups must put in place governance procedures that allow for potentially risky ventures when not all members are in support of such efforts. They must have processes of internal review, risk assessment, and constituency building among members.

- As they become more influential (and by necessity, controversial) players on the national scene, these affinity groups must be prepared to clearly articulate and defend their role as investors and change agents.

Foundation Support Centers

Just as important as the regional and national infrastructure organizations are the nonprofit support centers and for-profit consulting groups that are helping to train and build the capacity of newer foundations. Such entities can instill the value of collaboration at the earliest stages of a foundation's evolution, paving the way for a multitude of collaborative strategies.

An outstanding example is The Foundation Incubator (TFI). In Palo Alto, where there has been exponential growth in the number of small foundations, TFI was established to support their development. Structured as a membership organization, where members pay dues according to their asset size, TFI provides a range of services to new funders: shared administration function, office space, and meeting facilities; a cadre of experienced philanthropic colleagues who can serve as mentors or coaches; and centralized facilitation for groupings of funders that wish to take collaborative action. These groups undertake joint grant review sessions, co-funding, and learning field trips.

Its approach is about creating a total learning environment for both established foundations and donors. "We see it as a twenty-first century approach," explains Elizabeth Bremner, president of TFI. "When people talk about philanthropy, they usually refer to established foundations. But there are many funding vehicles available today. We make a point of being value neutral. We're not growing new foundations, but fostering new ideas and approaches. We're rethinking how you approach philanthropy education. We create a structured, guided peer-learning environment with intentional networking between established foundations and individual donors."

In a broad sense, the incubator's approach is collaborative, and both co-funding and networking result naturally from the work. One funder is giving to a group in Tanzania because another funder has already done the due diligence. TFI is now coordinating its first funder collaborative and hopes to launch a new one every one or two years. TFI was not organized explicitly to operate collaboratives and manage pooled funds, but finds them to be an ideal way of providing a learning experience about the kinds of issues and compromises that arise when funders work together.

University-Based Philanthropic Research Centers

By establishing specialized research centers, universities are gradually taking their place among the infrastructure institutions of philanthropy. Included in this group are the USC Center for Philanthropy; the Center on Philanthropy at Indiana University; the National Center on Philanthropy at New York University; the RGK Center for Philanthropy and Community at the University of Texas; the Center for Philanthropy at Grand Valley State University; and the Center for the Study of Philanthropy at Columbia University.

A relatively new breed of institution, these research centers possess unique attributes that position them as potential convenors of funder collaboratives. Empirical and objective data, of the kind that such centers collect, can serve as a basis for structuring conversations and finding points of common interest. These research centers can then play numerous critical roles in fostering funder collaboratives:

- University-based researchers can collect data on important social issues, framing the conclusions in terms of their implications for collaborative funding.

- Academics can monitor funding patterns across private foundations and public agencies—spotlighting redundancies, gaps in funding, and opportunities for collaboration.

- Professors and instructors can educate a next generation of foundation leaders with an understanding and appreciation of collaboration as a philanthropic tool.

- The staff of such research centers can actually convene and also staff funder collaboratives, especially those focused on practice-based learning. The staff can play a principal role in helping the funders to interpret and learn from their experiences.

Community Foundations

Community foundations have always represented natural staging grounds for funder collaboratives in that they exist as places to aggregate many philanthropic funds and are required to maintain extensive fund accounting systems to ensure the segregation of these monies. But their capacity to catalyze funder collaboratives differs enormously by city and region.

In more than a few locations, community foundations are perceived less as neutral intermediaries and more as individual foundations—driven by a single set of goals they have adopted and propelled by the personality and style of their presidents. Alternatively, they are viewed as the guardian and protector of each individual donor's insular vision. For community foundations to fulfill their potential as centers for funder collaboration, some will need to adopt some drastically different behaviors:

- Community foundation staff will need to hone their skills at helping individual donors rechannel their interest in leaving personal legacies behind toward more communal endeavors.

- Foundation staff will need to leave behind their role as personal advisors to donors and learn to convene individual donors as working groups capable of undertaking planned giving collectively.

- Foundation staff can promote the notion of "donor-advised funds for groups of foundations," offering administrative services for funder collaboratives (without necessarily participating as a member of the collaborative).

- Foundation staff can structure interactions between foundations and individual donors, helping them to understand the synergies and interdependencies that exist between them.

A Century from Now

If these infrastructure institutions rise to the challenge before them and re-engineer themselves to support the formation of funder collaboratives, what will this mean for the future of philanthropy? If the approaches of the three dozen or so funder collaboratives detailed in this book were expanded to their logical conclusions, how would philanthropy be transformed? If we view these illustrative examples as snapshots into a possible future, what would that future be?

A proliferation of funder collaboratives like the ones described herein would have dramatic effects on the nonprofit sector that include a more systematic organization and rationalization of the field; greater resources for planning and nonprofit restructuring across agencies; and capacity building that is of generalizable benefit. More predictable and aligned funding streams would result in higher efficiency ratios, which would in turn yield more impressive social outcomes.

Better outcomes would raise the bar for all philanthropic institutions in a virtuous cycle of higher standards. They would also re-energize the fields of social change that have suffered under the weight of high expectations and lackluster results for more than forty years. Funding could occur more rapidly and react to change and shifting issues more quickly. Just as the world is moving quicker, and changing more quickly, so must philanthropy. This new momentum could usher in a more optimistic era in which public belief in deliberate social change would rise.

The shift from unilateral "behind-closed-doors" decision making to collaborative multi-stakeholder processes would herald new experiments in democracy, with potential implications for both public sector and corporate governance. It could result in the stirrings of genuinely new and uniquely American democratic processes.

Finally, a widespread increase in the cohesion and level of organization in the philanthropic sector could raise its potency and stature as a professional field. Instead of an interesting and quaint outgrowth of capitalism, it could take its place as a counterpart to the public and private sectors, capable of leveraging change within each. Instead of a splintered set of uncoordinated acts of charity, philanthropy could mobilize and efficiently disburse capital flows in support of initiatives of unprecedented scale and significance.

David Brin, the renowned futurist and science fiction author, has envisioned a world in which philanthropic resources are coordinated and pooled in order to tackle much greater challenges than heretofore imagined. He recommends the creation of an institution that provides donors with a continually updated one-hundred-page catalogue of funding opportunities (each detailed according to cost, likelihood of success, degree of risk, and chance of sustainability). This fictitious institution, the Eye of the Needle (EON) Foundation, would then help organize the donors to collaboratively select and fund some of these options. The possibilities include a manned mission to Mars to be undertaken for $2.5 billion, or the creation of a Third World university network to be established for $5 billion.[2]

Such a glorified vision would most certainly have a flip side: An increasingly organized and effective philanthropy would no longer be able to operate below public radar screens or maintain perceptions of pure neutrality. Private foundations, and collaboratives of foundations, would be subject to considerable feedback, and even resistance, from organized networks in other sectors. They would be subject to a previously unseen level of public scrutiny and debate.

But in a very real sense, philanthropy would have achieved a new level of maturity. It would have taken its place as a formidable and fully actualized force among the institutions, sectors, and professions that shape the societies in which we live.

Notes

1. Bernholz, Lucy. *The Industry of Philanthropy: Highlights from Key Industry Analyses, 1999-2002.* San Francisco: Blueprint Research and Design, 14.
2. Brin, David, Ph.D. *The Future of Philanthropic Grantmaking: An Outsider's Perspective.* Copyright by David Brin, 2001.

Index

About the Author

After the 1992 civil unrest in Los Angeles, Mr. Hopkins was appointed Executive Director of Los Angeles Urban Funders (LAUF), housed at the Southern California Grantmakers. The foundation consortium was formed to mount an emergency response to the economic disparities underlying the riots. LAUF has carried out comprehensive neighborhood initiatives in three low-income geographic areas of Los Angeles and continues its operations today. Mr. Hopkins has helped other groups of funders in Southern California and elsewhere to replicate the approach.

Prior to LAUF Mr. Hopkins served as Assistant Director of the Mega-Cities Project, an international project based at the New York University Urban Research Center and funded by the World Bank, United Nations, Ford Foundation, Rockefeller Foundation, and other funding agencies. The project focused on the identification and replication of innovate solutions to problems that the world's cities face in common. In this capacity he worked with field-site teams based at urban research institutes in the largest cities worldwide, including Bangkok, Bombay, Cairo, Calcutta, Delhi, Istanbul, Jakarta, Lagos, Mexico City, Nairobi, Rio de Janeiro, São Paulo, and Tokyo.

Mr. Hopkins is currently the Founder and Managing Director of Emerging Markets, Inc., a consulting firm that assists financial institutions and other corporations to grow markets in low-income neighborhoods of Los Angeles. The firm utilizes a double bottom-line approach, assisting these institutions to carry out initiatives aimed at improving communities, while conducting profitable business within them.

An urban planner with a BA from Harvard University and MA in Urban and Regional Planning from UCLA, he has framed and executed major initiatives that have transformed low-income neighborhoods by connecting them to regional economic opportunities. His experiences have positioned him as a foremost thought leader advocating for progressive social change in cities. He speaks and publishes widely on the topic, guest lectures at universities in the United States and abroad, and has served as adviser to foundations, funding agencies, and corporations.

Mr. Hopkins's initiatives have been the subject of numerous case studies, articles, and documentaries and are the recipients of multiple awards for their cost-effectiveness, innovation, and leadership.